FACT OR FICTION?:
UFOs

FACT OR FICTION?:
UFOs

by

Nigel Blundell

Every effort has been made to trace the ownership of all copyright material and to secure permission from
copyright holders. In the event of any question arising as to the use of any material we will be pleased to
make the necessary corrections in future printings.

Photography with the kind permission of the Fortean Picture Library:
Pages: 11, 31 (top and bottom), 39 (top and bottom), 40, 41 (top), 45, 46 (top and bottom), 63,
66 (top and bottom), 76 (top and bottom), 85 (top and bottom), 86, 88 (top and bottom), 91, 95 (top and bottom).

CONTENTS

FACT OR FICTION

Ellen Crystal was an award-winning photographer and a PhD student of music at New York University when she saw him.

The setting was upstate New York, away from the lights and skyscrapers of the metropolis. That's where Ellen noticed the huge triangular craft wheeling in from the darkening night sky. Its sides were about 18 metres/60 feet long and it landed in a woodland copse not far from where she had parked. Ellen edged her car nearer . . . for a close encounter with an alien from another world.

He wore, she recalled, a tight-fitting beige suit, and was distinguished by his huge head, which had wrap-around yellow eyes going across it like a band. He was a tiny thing, little more than 120 cm/4 feet high, with no ears, a little bump for a nose and a slitty mouth. Her vision of the alien was brief. After being transfixed by her car beam he clambered back aboard his craft and soared away — back to his own world, wherever that might be.

This visitation in 1980 is just one of the many thousands that people have reported over the years: the arrival from unknown and uncharted worlds of beings who are just as curious about us as we are about them.

They have been represented in films and books as anything from little green men to HG Wells' *War of the Worlds* superbeings, intent on ravaging Earth. Whatever their purpose may be, can we really afford to dismiss every sighting claimed to be the work of an over-imaginative mind?

Obviously not. For the sheer weight of statistical evidence argues persuasively in favour of there being other forms of life in the universe.

In our galaxy alone there are 100,000 million stars, at least a fifth of them believed to be stable and relatively 'cool' like our Sun. About half of these stars are ringed with planets like those in our own solar system. It is likely that many of them are surrounded by an 'organic fog' containing the molecules that are the key to life.

So just what are the chances of there being life within our galaxy? If, as seems to be the case, 10,000 million stars have spawned associated planets, then the answer is: infinite!

The next question is: if there is life in space, why have we not yet encountered it?

The principal hopes for opening a channel of communication between ourselves and the stars lies in radio waves, which travel at very high speeds. The first methodical attempt to contact alien life forms via radio waves was made in 1960 when the 26 metre/85 feet wide aerial dish of the National Radio Observatory at Green Bank, West Virginia, was turned towards the stars Tau Ceti and Epsilon Eridani, only 11 light years away. After three months' constant monitoring, astronomers admitted that no signals from intelligent life had been picked up.

They announced philosophically: 'If we had found anything so close to Earth, it would have been a case of celestial overpopulation'.

The experiment, codenamed Project OZMA after the mythical Land of Oz, lapsed. But it became the forerunner of dozens of other projects to get the Earthlings' message into Outer Space.

The USA's 1972 Pioneer probe was allowed to spin off into space after completing its mission to explore Jupiter. On its side was a plaque bearing the pictures of a man and a woman, a coded message pinpointing planet Earth and hieroglyphics indicating that anyone finding the spacecraft should contact us on the 21 centimetre wavelength. It was the cosmic equivalent of a 'message in a bottle'. Additional, more sophisticated information was contained in the twin Voyager capsules sent to Mars in 1977. Similar messages, including video discs with everything from birdsongs to messages of greeting in 55 languages, have been sent up since.

Man's efforts to eavesdrop on space have also continued to proceed in an ever more methodical

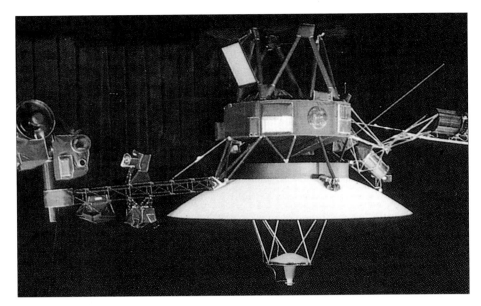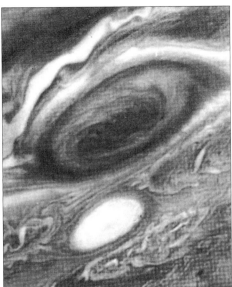

Voyager spacecraft – eyes and ears of the solar system (l)   The strange Great Red Spot on the surface of Jupiter (r)

manner. Microwave frequencies are being hunted by listening equipment at Harvard University, Massachusetts. A worldwide effort to co-ordinate radio telescopes has resulted in the monitoring of 70,000 consecutive radio channels. As computers maximise the effects of such monitoring, it is possible to listen in on no fewer than 10 million different frequencies.

The problem with such experiments is, of course, time and distance. The figures become virtually incomprehensible. For instance, radio waves travel at the speed of light. A light year is the distance that light travels in one year — about 10 million million kilometres/six million, million miles. So when we talk about stars like Tau Ceti and Epsilon Eridani being 'close' to Earth (only 12 light years distant) what we mean is that they are 116 billion kilometres/72 billion miles away!

To have a hope of reaching other galaxies, we must expect a radio message to take 20 to 30 years in simply travelling through space. And that means a reply would equally take the same number of decades to return to us.

The good news for interplanetary contact is that radio waves have been shooting away from Earth since the beginning of the century. It is those messages — and more recently television signals — that aliens would have first picked up.

The bad news is that, having seen and heard all about us, they may simply have decided not to return our calls.

And yet, while the radio waves remain silent, the skies have been filled with alien visitations — Unidentified Flying Objects – not just recently, but since the beginning of recorded history. One of the myths of modern science is that UFOs are a recent phenomenon. But there is nothing new in tales of alien sightings. Ever since primitive man first drew himself upright and stared at the heavens, he has pondered the eternal question: is there life out there?

It is in this century, though, that accelerating advances in science have encouraged us to think we may soon have an answer. New technology, spreading populations, increased awareness and heightened vigilance have all combined to give us a clearer pattern of possible alien activity and UFO visitations. A greater readiness to come forward and report a UFO sighting has also added to the breadth of knowledge accumulated on the subject.

Those who have not seen a UFO remain, like the biblical Thomas, doubting.

But anyone who has actually seen one — or more dramatically, had a close encounter with one — will never forget the experience. For many, as in the case of Ellen Crystal and of others catalogued in this book, it has changed their lives forever.

WORLDWIDE ENCOUNTERS

Encounters Of The First Kind

'Sighting of an Unidentified Flying Object in the immediate vicinity'

– Dr J Allen Hynek, Centre For UFO Studies, Evanston, Illinois

FLYING SAUCER MAN

Businessman Kenneth Arnold always kept his eyes open for money-making opportunities. So when he heard there was a 5000 dollar reward for the finder of a crashed US Marine transport plane, there was no stopping him.

He was an experienced pilot, with more than 4000 hours' flying experience, and was flying to Yakima, Washington that afternoon, anyway. The US Marine Curtess C-46 had gone down a couple of months earlier, somewhere near the 4400 m/14,400 ft plateau of Mount Rainier. Arnold reckoned he would be able to spend an hour or so searching the area on the way. He took off from Chehalis, Washington, at about 2 pm on 24 June 1947, and flew straight into the pages of UFO history.

Arnold had every reason to feel confident as he started out. His own plane, a single-engined Callier, was specially designed for work in the mountains and was capable of landing on the roughest terrain. It was a bright, sunny day. Perfect search weather.

He took the plane up to 2750 metres/9000 feet and began his search. He was completing a 180 degree turn over the town of Mineral when a bright flash shot across his wings and fuselage.

Arnold's heart skipped a beat. He thought he had just had a near miss with another aircraft and began searching the skies frantically trying to identify it and avoid a collision.

He spotted a DC-4 in the distance behind him, but it was too far off to have caused the flash. He began to assume he had been buzzed by a USAF P-51 fighter. Then there was a second flash.

This time Arnold was able to see the source. From the north, near Mount Baker, was a tight formation of nine very bright objects. Judging from their apparent speed, they were jet fighters. He estimated them to be about 160 km/100 miles away and they were coming in his direction.

'They were flying in an echelon formation with a larger gap in their echelon between the first four and the last five,' Arnold told reporters later. 'They didn't fly like any aircraft I had seen before. In the first place, their echelon formation was the reverse of that practised by our air force. The elevation of the first craft was greater than that of the last. They flew in a definite formation, but erratically.

'Their flight was like that of speedboats on rough water or similar to the tail of a Chinese kite that I once saw blowing in the wind. Or maybe it would be best to describe their flight characteristics as being very similar to a formation of geese, in a rather diagonal chain-like line. They fluttered and sailed, tipping their wings alternately and emitting those very bright blue-white flashes from their surfaces.

'At the time, I did not get the impression these flashes were emitted by them, but rather that it was the sun's reflection from the extremely polished surface of their wings'.

He watched as they closed on him. At their closest, they were about 32 km/20 miles away. One of the craft looked different from the rest: darker and crescent-shaped. What astonished him most was that none of the 'aircraft' had tails. Using the known distance between the peaks of Mount Rainier and Mount Adams as a yardstick, Arnold attempted to use his dashboard clock to time the UFOs' passage so he could work out their speed, which he judged to be around 2100 km/1300 miles per hour. He was also able to calculate the formation's length at about 8 km/5 miles.

He watched until the objects disappeared from sight, then raced to land at Yakima where he sped into the office of Al Baxter, boss of Central Aircraft and told him what he had seen. Baxter listened and watched as Arnold drew pictures of the flying objects. Unable to offer a rational explanation, he called in his helicopter instructors and pilots for their opinions.

One of them dismissed Arnold's story with: 'Ah, it's just a flight of those guided missiles from Moses Lake'.

Arnold took off again, this time for Pendleton, Oregon. Yakima radioed ahead and passed on his story. So by the time Arnold touched down again there were plenty of people waiting to hear what he had seen.

$2.50

The COMING of the SAUCERS

By Kenneth Arnold & Ray Palmer

At this point, Arnold decided it was time to call on the FBI. He suspected the objects might have been Russian aircraft which had entered US airspace via the Polar route. So he went to the local FBI office, only to find it closed. He ended up telling to the story to the East Oregonian newspaper, from where it was passed on to the Associated Press.

'They flew like a saucer would if you skipped it across water', Arnold told journalists, and the phrase 'flying saucer' was born. It captured public imagination all around the globe.

Arnold was undoubtedly a credible witness in the popular view. He was president of a company which made fire extinguishers and also an acting deputy US marshall. But some scientists were later to question his estimates of speed and distance. If he had been mistaken, the objects may have been smaller and much closer to him than he thought. They would also have been travelling much more slowly — perhaps at conventional airspeeds. Sceptics suggest it may have been nothing more than a flock of birds, as indeed many suspected UFOs turn out to be.

A more recent theory is that Arnold was a witness to so-called 'earth lights': glowing balls of electro-magnetic energy thought to be released along fault lines in the planet's crust. There is no evidence to suggest the truth or otherwise of this. By contrast, however, Arnold's drawings of the objects he saw are extremely birdlike, with two swept back wings and no tail section. They were not saucers at all – Arnold was describing their style of flight, not their appearance, when he made his 'flying saucer' comment.

That did not matter to the public at large. Between June and July of that year, there were some 850 reported UFO sightings across the United States. Among them was one from a prospector called Johnson who claimed to have seen five or six discs in the Cascade Mountains area on the same day as Arnold. It was clear the newspaper stories about had sparked a tidal wave.

'I could have gone to sleep that night if reporters, newsmen and press agencies of every description had left me alone', Arnold wrote later. 'I didn't share the general excitement. I can't begin to estimate the number of people, letters, telegrams and phone calls I tried to answer. After three days of this hubbub, I came to the conclusion that I was the only sane one in the bunch. In order to stop what I thought was a lot of foolishness, and since I couldn't get any work done, I went out to the airport, cranked up my plane and flew home to Boise'.

But there was no escape for Doris and Kenneth Arnold. Even at home they were besieged by television crews and reporters. Later, as people tired of the UFO madness, Arnold found himself on the receiving end again. This time he was dismissed as a nutcase.

'Nameless, faceless people ridiculed me', he said shortly before his death in 1984. 'I was considered an Orson Welles, a fraud. I loved my country. I was very naive about the whole thing. I was the unfortunate goat who first reported them'.

Arnold's 'flying saucer' sighting was only the first of many he was to have during his life, a fact some cynics have pounced upon. In 1952, he saw two objects, one of which appeared transparent. It was his eighth encounter since the Mount Rainier sighting.

He said later: 'They looked like something alive. I've had the feeling with these things that they are aware of me but they make no effort to come close'.

In 1966 he captured an object on cine film over Idaho Falls, Ohio. It looked similar to a weather balloon, but was travelling into the wind.

The most resounding evidence in Arnold's favour are the words of an FBI agent who quizzed him in 1947 after the first incident. The agent wrote: 'It is also the opinion of the interviewer that [Arnold] would have much more to lose than gain and would have to be very strongly convinced that he actually saw something before he would report such an incident and open himself up for the ridicule that accompanies such a report'.

WORLDWIDE SIGHTINGS

The Arnold sighting set the world ablaze. From Tokyo to London, New York to Nepal, reports of strange lights in the sky, flying discs and cigar-shaped objects meant civil and military investigators had their hands full. Newspaper editors and radio stations were desperate for anything they could get on the news sensation of 1947. Hoaxers had a field day, but some stories could not simply be written off.

The sightings began in North America but spread rapidly around the globe. By the mid-1950s, there were few places that had not reported close encounters.

Four days after Arnold made his famous 'flying saucer' remark, a US Air Force pilot flying an F-51 near Lake Meade, Nevada, reported that he had seen five or six circular objects off his right wing. They were flying in close formation.

The same evening four USAF officers, two intelligence men and two pilots, saw a brilliant light which was zig-zagging across the sky over Montgomery, Alabama. It made an amazing 90 degree turn before zooming off.

A few days later, on the morning of 4 June 1947, a carload of people driving near Redmond, Oregon, saw four flying discs speed past Mount Jefferson. At 1.05 pm, a policeman in the car park behind nearby Portland City police HQ saw five large disc-shaped objects overhead. Two other cops, themselves former pilots, and four harbour patrolmen were among dozens of Portlanders who saw similar objects at approximately the same time.

That night, two United Airlines pilots were flying from Boise, Idaho to Seattle, Washington. At a height of about 2450 metres/8000 feet, they saw what appeared to be several light aircraft in front of them. When Captain Emil J Smith turned on his landing lights to see better, he and co-pilot Ralph Stevens were amazed to see a formation of large grey discs.

They called the stewardess, who confirmed what they had seen. Capt Smith called the tower at Ontario, Oregon, and asked for a radar check. Controllers there could not track the objects and Capt Smith made up his mind that they had to be much further away and even larger than he had originally suspected. The objects appeared to melt together and disappeared into the north-west.

Two days later, the crew of a US Air Force B-25 in the same area saw another disc below them. And in California, near Fairfield-Suisun airbase, a pilot caught a fleeting glimpse of a spinning disc as it shot across the sky.

The episode which most disturbed US defence chiefs happened on 8 July, above the top secret Muroc airbase (now Edwards), later to be the home of the legendary Bell-X rocket planes. At 10 am a test pilot saw what he thought was a weather balloon — until he realised it was travelling against the wind. Other airmen on the base had seen similar objects earlier that day. Two hours later, a ground crew on Rogers Dry Lake saw a round, white object which seemed to be constructed of aluminium approach a formation of P-82 and A-26 experimental aircraft.

The planes were carrying out a test on ejector seats and, as an ejected dummy fell to earth, the object followed it down. The object had no visible propulsion system and was totally silent. Four hours later, a flat, grey flying disc was spotted by an F-51 aircraft travelling at 6000 metres/20,000 feet. It then climbed rapidly out of the fighter's range.

In another sighting, on 2 July 1948, ten people witnessed eight UFOs pass over the town of Disma, Idaho and land fleetingly on a nearby hill. On the same day, a similar formation was seen over Augusta, Maine. When various other reports were collated, it emerged that UFOs had been seen at the same time in no less than 33 North american statesn states.

Within days of the original Arnold sighting, there had been copycat cases in South America, most notably in the Bauru region of Brazil where a UFO had allegedly landed and its crew attempted to lure

FACT OR FICTION?: UFOs

Shuttle: buzzed by UFOs (top)   Apollo 11: astronauts 'saw UFOs' (bottom)

a forestry worker inside it. But the first incident to be taken seriously came at Lego Argentino, Argentina, on 18 March, 1950. Rancher Wilfredo Arevalo watched while a UFO touched down, guarded by a second machine hovering close overhead. Arevalo walked to within 122 metres/400 feet of the craft and noticed an intense smell of something like benzene. The craft took off after a few minutes, leaving an area of scorched grass behind it.

UFOs had been frequent visitors to Europe in the years immediately after the Second World War, most notably in the shape of 'ghost rockets' seen over Scandinavia. After the Arnold sighting, all hell broke loose on both sides of the Iron Curtain.

The encounter of headmaster Monsieur Prigent in October 1952 was one such. He, along with his wife and children, saw a curiously-shaped cloud in the skies over his home in Oldron-Sainte-Marie. Behind it was a long cylinder which seemed to be emitting an exhaust trail. Ahead of it were some 30 disc-shaped UFOs which left a trail of so-called 'angel hair' behind them.

In July 1953, a group of five Poles and two Germans watched in amazement as a saucer-shaped object hovered next to a railway line near Wolin Island, Szczecin in Poland. Estimated at 18 metres/60 feet across, it touched down only momentarily before zooming off.

Royal Air Force pilots testified to numerous encounters over the North Sea and the Thames Estuary during the early 1950s. In October 1954 Flight Lieutenant James Salandin was flying a Meteor jet fighter at 4900 metres/16,000 feet over Southend when he saw three objects heading straight for him. They split up as they reached him and then zoomed off. He described them as being disc-shaped and as having a central sphere.

'The things were right in my sights', he said later. 'Next time I'll be on the ball'.

There were other such sightings in Spain, Belgium, France and Germany.

Rome was thrown into turmoil when in November 1954 what appeared to be a fleet of UFOs buzzed the city at an estimated 1290 km/800 miles per hour. Hundreds of people saw the white dots flashing across the sky, among them leading Italian politician Dr Alberto Perego.

Africa too was not immune. In July 1954, a Tiger Moth piloted by instructor Squadron Leader A Roberts was being flown near Lake McIlwaine in what was then Rhodesia. Roberts and his students saw a flying disc, about 12 metres/40 feet in diameter and approximately 2.5 km/1½ miles above them. It turned on its side and sped off.

This brief casebook of early encounters was enough to convince many people within the armed forces of the need to further investigate UFO sightings. The in-fighting between those who believed and those who did not was to supply the public with a rich and confusing diet of information throughout the next three decades.

FLYING NIGHTMARES

Military pilots the world over have confronted Unidentified Flying Objects. While their 'top brass' often deny the existence of such things, mess-room gossip tells a different story. To air crews, an Unidentified Flying Object presents an immediate threat because its intentions are unknown — and taking the correct evasive or offensive action could be a matter of life and death.

The evidence of pilots who have encountered UFOs is particularly convincing. They are highly-skilled men, whose intense training demands a cool-headed, rational approach to the unexpected. Their reports speak repeatedly of disc-shaped objects flying at phenomenal speeds: up to 15,000 km/9000 miles per hour or more.

Flying instruments habitually go dead as the UFO draws closer and weapons systems fail. The first recorded death of a flyer chasing a UFO came on 8 January 1948, when control tower staff at Goodman Field, Kentucky, spotted a mysterious disc-shaped object in the sky. One hour later, Captain Thomas Mantell and his flight of P-51 Mustangs were ordered to divert from their planned route and investigate.

They began climbing towards the object. None of the planes were equipped with oxygen for use at high altitude and three of them turned back at 4600 metres/15,000 feet. Mantell continued, however. His last transmission said he had the object in sight and was still climbing.

Minutes later, he was dead. Wreckage from his aircraft was scattered over a mile. The official report says that Mantell was chasing a Skyhook weather balloon and that he blacked out as a result of oxygen deficiency. Evidence suggests the aircraft broke up as it fell out of the sky.

In September 1952 a major Nato exercise in the North Sea was disrupted by a series of UFO sightings. On 19 September, the five-man crew of an RAF Meteor jet were buzzed by a 'silver and circular' object over Dishforth in Yorkshire.

Two days later, a flight of six RAF jets saw a similar object over the sea. They began to pursue it, but it accelerated out of sight. It returned to play 'tag' with another Meteor before disappearing again.

Later the same year, a USAF bomber flying over the Gulf of Mexico picked up a blip moving at more than 8000 km/5000 miles per hour. As the B-29 crew, led by Captain John Harter, checked for possible radar malfunctions, they discovered the original UFO had been joined by three others. Six minutes after the first contact, they watched awe-struck as the objects speed past the starboard side of the plane in a blue-white streak.

A second group of objects then homed in on the plane, slowed down and shadowed it from close range for more than ten seconds before they too sped off. Moments later a huge UFO appeared and appeared to dock with the smaller craft — all still moving at 8000 km/5000 miles per hour. The mother ship then accelerated to 15,000 km/9000 miles per hour before disappearing off the radar.

In early 1953, Flight Lieutenant Cyril Townsend-Withers was flying an RAF Canberra jet at 17,000 metres/55,000 feet over Salisbury Plain. He spotted a silver disc in the sky and his radar confirmed a solid object in that position. The aircraft attempted to close in but the object flew upwards at 90 degrees at a fantastic speed.

Another UFO sighting in July 1954 ended tragically when an F-94 jet crashed near Walesville, New York State, after pursuing an unidentified radar contact. The crew clearly saw a gleaming, disc-shaped object hanging motionless in the sky and climbed towards it. They radioed it for an identification but there was no response. Instead their instruments blacked out and the cockpit began to heat up, although there was no other indication of a fire on board.

The navigator and the pilot both baled out before the aircraft nose-dived into the ground, killing two children and two adults.

In August 1956, two RAF Venom jets were launched to investigate a radar contact over

Captain Thomas Mantell: struck down by alien force ?

Cambridgeshire. The first pilot locked on to the contact and then watched in amazement as it turned and began tailing him. The MoD has never released gun camera film of the incident but its existence has been admitted by Ralph Noyes, the civil servant who took over the ministry's UFO department in 1969.

There have been incidents in every corner of the globe. In the early 1970s a French minister revealed that their air force had pursued numerous UFOs and would continue to do so. Sardinia was the location for a sighting by Major Francesco Zoppi of the Italian Air Corps. He was on a normal helicopter training flight in October 1977 when a bright, orange object appeared and began shadowing his aircraft. After a few moments, it disappeared at enormous speed. The object was also seen by observers on the ground.

In 1982, a flight of Chinese fighters patrolling the Heilong Jiang province closed in on a strange yellow-green light in the sky which was roughly the size of the full moon. As they closed, their electrical systems went haywire, leaving them without navigational or communication links. They were forced to return to base. One encounter in particular is worthy of special attention. It took place in the skies over Iran in September 1976, when just after midnight the Imperial Iranian Air Force took calls from people in Teheran saying they had seen a strange bird-like object hovering above the city.

An F-4 fighter was scrambled from Shahrokhi base about an hour later. The object was so bright that it could be seen from 112 km/70 miles away. As the fighter closed to 48 km/30 miles, the pilot's navigation and communications systems went dead – but as soon as he turned towards his home base to land, the system returned to normal.

A second fighter was scrambled and this time it managed to lock its radar on the target from about 52 km/32 miles out. As the range came down to about 48 km/30 miles, the object turned and sped off. The fighter continued to pursue the UFO, which was now flashing blue, green, red and orange.

The radar blip suggested it was the size of a medium airliner. Suddenly another object appeared to come out of the first and head straight for the fighter, who attempted to fire an AIM-9 missile. At that moment, his navigational, communications and weapons systems went dead. The pilot went into a crash-dive to escape, only to find the newcomer had rejoined the mother ship. A third object now broke off from the first and headed at incredible speed towards the earth.

The crew expected to see an explosion but instead saw a bright ring of light below where the object appeared to have made a safe landing. They noted the position and returned to base, suffering several communications blackouts as they returned.

Observers on the ground had managed to locate at least one of the objects on their radar. The 'landing site' was investigated the following day and locals said they had seen strange lights in the sky and heard a loud noise, like an explosion.

The incident was subsequently investigated by both the Iranian and US military, and stood up under the closest scrutiny. To date, there have been no reports of UFOs opening fire on military aircraft. What might happen if a pilot managed to shoot one down can only be guessed at.

UFOs OVER WASHINGTON

Veteran pilots William Nash and William Fortenberry couldn't believe their eyes. High above Washington DC, their Miami-bound Pan-Am DC-4 was being buzzed by half-a-dozen flying discs. At first the UFOs flew beneath the aircraft, then they shot across the sky at crazy angles, soared upwards and vanished out of sight. It was 8.12 pm on 14 July 1952 and the biggest UFO scare in North American history was about to begin.

Five days later at about 11.40 pm, Air Route Traffic Control (ARTC) at Washington National Airport picked up a formation of seven unidentified objects slightly south-east of Andrews airbase outside the city. The blips seemed to be aircraft travelling at about 200 km/125 miles per hour — until two of them accelerated and sped off the radar screens at an estimated 11,000 km/700 mph. The radars were checked within minutes and were found to be in perfect working order.

At the same time, crews of several airliners in the area reported mysterious lights crossing their flight-paths. Eye-witnesses on the ground confirmed the sightings. Even the colours of the objects were agreed upon: orange, changing to green, to red.

Radar officer Howard Cocklin looked out of the Washington National control tower himself and could see a bright light in the sky where one of the blips should have been. Elsewhere, an off-duty airman phoned nearby Andrews airbase after seeing an orange ball of fire in the sky. The officer he spoke to stepped out of his office and saw it too, directly above him.

At 1 am a Capital airline DC-4 piloted by Captain Casey Pierman was directed towards the intruders by radar control and spotted several lights in the sky. As the plane approached, the lights zoomed off.

Captain Pierman said later: 'In all my years of flying, I've seen a lot of falling or shooting stars, but these were much faster than anything like that I've ever seen. They couldn't have been aircraft . . . they were moving too fast.'

Panic set in when two of the objects broke away and began flying down the no-go zone over the White House while another hovered over the Capitol. Chief radar controller Harry Barnes decided to call Air Force High Command but it was not until 3 am that two F-94 interceptors finally reached the area.

By that time, other aircraft were reporting strange lights bouncing around the sky all over the city. When the jets showed up, the lights shot off again. It was if the blips had been monitoring the fighter planes' radio transmissions.

The chaos went on until dawn. At least one of the strange objects was simultaneously tracked by two radar stations at Washington's National Airport and by a third at Maryland airbase, three miles north of the city.

There were other sightings that night, too, with reports of lights in the sky over Newport News in Virginia. Another interceptor was launched when lights were seen over nearby Langley Field airbase. The base control tower guided the plane until the UFO was in sight and then it disappeared — in the words of the pilot, 'just as if someone had turned out the light.' The pilot continued to track the target using radar but eventually lost it. By the time he landed again at Langley Field, the objects had reappeared over Washington.

The next night, radar tracked more UFOs as they performed what an Air Force weather observer described as extraordinary 'gyrations and reversals'. They were moving at more than 1440 km/900 miles per hour and radar echoes suggested they were solid objects.

The Pentagon's reaction — just like the launch of the first fighter planes — was slow and stumbling. Officially, its approach was 'no comment'. Eventually, it agreed to let Captain Edward J Ruppelt of Project Blue Book investigate the sightings. Blue Book had been set up earlier that year by the USAF to check out the flying saucer phenomenon. Many had thought it little more than a public relations exercise.

UFO formation over the White House: reported by dozens of eyewitnesses on 19 July 1952

Ruppelt was given written orders to visit the city for one day, and was reminded that he would be classed AWOL if he stayed any longer. He was denied a staff car and the expense chits he submitted for a hired vehicle were refused. Ruppelt tired of this, rang his boss at the Pentagon to complain – and ended up catching the next plane back to his home base in Dayton, Ohio.

'I decided that if saucers were buzzing Pennsylvania Avenue in formation, I couldn't care less', he said.

The sightings continued all that week and erupted in a frenzy the following weekend. This time three Blue Book officers were rushed to Washington Airport's operations room and were in time to see most of the blips. Two F-94 interceptors were launched and the Blue Book men were in constant radio contact with them.

Again, when the jets reached the target zone the blips and the lights vanished. They turned up at Langley, Virginia — home of the CIA — where a USAF jet and several witnesses on the ground saw them.

The interceptors left Washington. The UFOs returned. More F-94s were sent up. This time, one of the pilots got a radar lock on one of the blips. As he closed in, the UFO accelerated to an incredible speed and so was able to escape.

Another pilot, Lieutenant William Patterson, managed to get a sighting of one UFO and kicked in his afterburner to pursue it as it sped off. He was ten miles away when it suddenly backtracked and, with others that appeared seemingly from nowhere, surrounded him in seconds. Badly shaken, the pilot radioed Andrews airbase and asked if he should open fire. After a tense moment, the UFOs sped off into space again.

The US Air Force's response after a whole week of sightings was just like the Pentagon's. At one of the biggest press conferences it had held since World War II, it put forward the theory that the sightings had been mirages caused by 'temperature inversion' in the upper atmosphere. None of the F-94 pilots were present. None of the radar officers were present. Instead a radar expert who had met none of the witnesses was flown in to argue for the mirage theory.

Project Blue Book simply recorded the incidents as 'unexplained'.

The shock of the sightings was to have major repercussions within the US defence establishment. The CIA's H Marshall Chadwell feared the Soviets might have been behind the affair and pointed out that UFO stories could be planted to create mass hysteria and panic. Indeed, the sightings had clogged US intelligence channels. Had the Soviets launched an air or missile strike, there would have been no way for the appropriate warnings to get through.

As a result, the CIA approached Project Blue Book and said it wanted to 'review' all data gathered on UFOs since 1947. A CIA physicist subsequently produced a report which dismissed Blue Book's work , and suggesting more should be done to debunk them. Project Blue Book was effectively downgraded.

Fifteen years later, the National Airport radar officers were again quizzed on the so-called Washington Flap, this time by experts from the University of Colorado. They stuck to their story. To this day, few UFO sightings have been so well documented, or witnessed by so many people.

The US Air Force's official investigation into UFOs worked through numerous code names during the 1940s and early 1950s. It had started out as Project Sign in 1948, becoming Project Grudge in 1950 and Project Blue Book in 1952. Its full name was the Aerial Phenomena Group.

The group was launched on 22 January 1948, a few days after the mysterious death of USAF Captain Thomas Mantell. He had been piloting an F-51 aircraft chasing an unidentified silvery object which was also seen by observers on the ground near Godman Field, Kentucky. His last words suggested the object had been closing in on him. The wreckage of his plane was found some hours later.

Project Sign/Blue Book staff included technicians and scientists as well as intelligence officers. When Captain Ruppelt took over there was a split among air force officers, some who believed UFOs were pure fantasy, others who thought there was a genuine threat from aliens or foreign powers against the US. It was, after all, the height of the Cold War.

Public interest in UFOs was undeniable, with numerous films being made on the subject and hundreds of magazines and comic strips taking flying saucers for their theme.

One particularly controversial article appeared in *Life* magazine in March 1952, just as Project Blue Book began its work. Headlined *Have We Visitors From Outer Space?* it included quotes allegedly from key defence figures saying things like: 'Maybe they're interplanetary'.

Once the CIA became involved after the Washington Flap, the over-riding aim of government research seems to have been the debunking of the UFO mystery. It was even suggested that Walt Disney make a movie on the subject to put people's minds at rest.

Captain Ruppelt quit the air force in 1953 to write his controversial memoirs, published two years later. In them he reflects: 'Maybe I was just the front man for a big cover-up'.

One-time US president Jimmy Carter launched a $20 million study into UFOs

FACT OR FICTION?: UFOs

While he was president of the United States, Jimmy Carter launched a $20 million study into UFOs. The reason for his enthusiasm could well have been an experience in 1973 when he was still governor of Georgia. Carter and 20 other people had just completed an official dinner and had stepped out onto the balcony of a mansion at Thomastown. In his own words: 'We witnessed an object which looked as big as the moon and changed colour several times from red to green and back again'.

In the same year another governor, Ohio's John Gilligan, reported seeing a UFO near Ann Arbor, Michigan, describing it as 'a vertical shaft of light which glowed amber'.

US governmental agencies have instituted several investigations into UFO activity, but they have been so faint-hearted that little has been achieved. In 1978 an attempt was made to have the United Nations officially investigate UFOs. The unsuccessful bid was made by John Gilligan, Prime Minister of the Caribbean island of Grenada, who said that he himself had witnessed one. 'It was a brilliant golden light travelling at tremendous speed', he said.

German-born actress Elke Sommer is a celebrity who seems to have gained one of the clearest UFO sightings. She was in the garden of her Los Angeles home in 1978 when an orange ball of light hovered above the house. She said: 'It appeared out of the blue and was about 20 feet in diameter. It was glowing and floating about like a great moon. It came towards me and I fled into the house. When I reappeared, it had vanished'.

It is rare for a UFO to appear over such a highly populated area as Los Angeles. But few places are as crowded as New York's Manhattan Island — and that is where boxer Mohammed Ali witnessed a UFO while he was on a training session through Central Park in 1972. 'I was out jogging just before sunrise when this bright light hovered over me. It just seemed to be watching me. It was like a huge electric light-bulb in the sky'.

MYSTERIOUS ENCOUNTERS

THE ROSWELL INCIDENT

The day's work was coming to an end for ranch foreman Mac Brazel as he rode out to move a flock of sheep from one field to another. With him was one of the neighbour's sons, Tim Proctor. It was 3 July 1947, a fortnight after Kenneth Arnold's sensational sighting of 'flying saucers', and America was in the grip of UFO fever.

As Brazel and his companion rode across the desert outside Corona, New Mexico, they came upon a trail of strange metallic debris. It was spread up and down the hillsides and there was a large gouge in the earth. It looked as if an aircraft had crashed and exploded.

Many UFOlogists believe that what they had stumbled upon was the first solid evidence that flying saucers might be extra-terrestrial in origin. For his part, Brazel automatically linked the wreckage with a loud bang he had heard the night before and had attributed to thunder – there had been a violent rainstorm in the area.

The pieces of metal were like nothing he or Tim had ever seen. They were pliable. They were very light and reverted to their original shape even after being crunched into a ball. Some pieces had odd markings on them. Brazel was unaware that there had been a UFO sighting over Roswell, 120 km/75 miles away, the night before. The object's flight path would have taken it right over the wreck site.

What happened in the aftermath of the discovery has been the inspiration for numerous films and books since. Some researchers are convinced that not only was wreckage found, but also the bodies of the alien beings who manned the craft.

Brazel took samples of debris into Roswell town on 6 July and presented them at the sheriff's office. Two deputies were immediately ordered to the crash site but could not find it. They did however come across a patch of scorched ground as if something had landed there.

Brazel was meanwhile ordered to the nearby Roswell air base, where intelligence officer Major Jesse Marcel and junior officer Sheridan Cavitt drove him out to Corona, loaded more of the wreckage on to a pick-up truck and took it back to the base the following day. The metal samples Brazel had brought in earlier were sent to Carswell air base in Fort Worth, Texas, for expert analysis. Next day Brazel met air force security at the crash site and they cordoned it off — even to the local police.

The rest of the wreckage was loaded up and taken back to Roswell airbase along with Brazel, who found himself under 'voluntary' house arrest for a week. He never spoke about the crash site in public again. Roswell commander Colonel William Blanchard ordered Marcel to load up a B-29 bomber and fly the wreckage to Wright Patterson airbase in Dayton, Ohio, stopping at Carswell on the way to pick up the samples. Ground crew who loaded the plane were amazed at how light the crates were considering how much wreckage there was.

Blanchard then put out a statement on the wires which ran like this:

'The many rumours regarding the flying discs became a reality yesterday when the intelligence office of the 509th bomb group of the 8th air force, Roswell Army Air Field, was fortunate enough to gain possession of a disc through the co-operation of one of the local ranchers and the sheriff's office at Chaves county. The flying object landed on a ranch near Roswell some time last week. Not having phone facilities, the rancher stored the disc until such time as he was able to contact the sheriff's office, who in turn notified Major Jesse A Marcel of the 509th bomb group intelligence office. It was inspected at the Roswell Army Air Field and subsequently loaned by Major Marcel to higher headquarters'.

It was then that sinister things began to happen. As the wire story was coming in over the teletype to a radio station in Albuquerque, it was interrupted by a further message reading: 'Attention Albuquerque: Cease transmission. Repeat: cease transmission. National security item. Do not transmit . . .'

At this point all transmission stopped.

Meanwhile, Marcel had landed at Carswell and been virtually thrown off the plane by General Roger Ramey, who took immediate command, told Marcel to keep silent on the affair and fly back to Roswell at once. Ramey then issued a second press statement, saying the wreckage was that of a weather balloon, and arranged a hurried press conference at which debris from a Rawin weather balloon was produced. It has since emerged that Commander Ramey, who had so forcefully taken charge, was under direct orders from the Pentagon to 'put out the fire' over Roswell.

Nothing emerged to challenge this story until the mid-1970s when Stanton T Friedman, a physicist, tracked down two witnesses who had been in New Mexico in 1947. He persuaded them to talk about what they had seen. One was the girl in the radio station who had seen the teletype machine and the two messages from Roswell airbase. The other was Major Marcel, who was now retired, who had been the first intelligence officer to see the wreckage.

He stated flatly that its material of could not be of earthly origin. His description of the wreckage makes fascinating reading. He recalled: 'We found . . . all sorts of stuff: small beams about 1 cm or $1\frac{1}{2}$ cm square (⅜ or ½ inch square) with some sort of hieroglyphics on them which nobody could decipher. These looked something like balsa wood and were of about the same weight, although flexible, and would not burn.

'There was a great deal of an unusual parchment-like substance which was brown in colour and extremely strong, and a great number of small pieces of a metal like tin foil, except that it wasn't tin foil. The parchment writing had little numbers and symbols that we had to call hieroglyphics because we could not understand them. They were pink and purple. They looked like they were painted on. These little numbers could not be broken, could not be burned – wouldn't even smoke.'

When an acetylene torch was turned on to one sample, it barely warmed up and was cold to the touch seconds later. Even a sledgehammer could not make a mark upon it. Lieutenant Colonel Arthur Exon, who became base commander at Wright-Patterson in the 1960s and who was serving on the base in 1947, said later: 'The overall consensus was that the pieces were from space'.

UFOs seem to be attracted to areas around atomic installations and military bases, particularly those in the area known as the Texas Triangle. Its sides are each about 290 km/180 miles long and stretch between Lubbock and Alpine in Texas and Albuquerque in New Mexico.

The Roswell wreckage was found only 160 km/100 miles south of the Los Alamos atomic research station and a few miles north of the White Sands and Alamogordo atomic weapon ranges. At the height of the Cold War, these were highly sensitive sites. And Roswell airbase was the only one in the world at that time with an active bomber squadron carrying atomic weapons.

Two years after the Roswell incident, on 24 April 1949, a UFO was spotted over White Sands Proving Grounds by a US Navy team tracking a weather balloon they had launched. One of the team, Charles Moore, spotted a white, egg-shaped object in the sky. It was seen by his colleagues and they continued to track it for more than a minute.

Their data suggests the UFO was travelling at 11 km/7 miles per second — the velocity required to overcome earth's gravity — and was approximately 90 km/56 miles high. At one point the object made an 80 degree turn which, at that speed, would have killed any human aboard it. Another UFO was seen in 1957 just south of Alamogordo, New Mexico, near the site of the first atomic explosion, which took place there in 1945.

A photograph of the object – taken by Ella Fortune – remains a matter of controversy, with some dismissing it as a weather balloon or an unusual cloud formation. Could it be that UFOs were somehow policing the Cold War, preventing either the United States or the Soviet Union from launching a nuclear strike? This would explain their apparent interest in defence sites.

Evidence to support the theory comes from a mysterious explosion at a secret Soviet defence plant in 1952, reported in The UFO Phenomenon by Johannes Von Buttlar. For a week before the blast, several cigar-shaped and disc-shaped objects had been seen in the sky above the area. Then at dawn one morning, witnesses saw a huge fireball descend on the factory.

There was a loud explosion and the section of the plant which made missile-firing devices was reduced to rubble. After the blast, a disc was seen hovering over the site for several minutes but was chased off by fighter planes. Soviet authorities blamed United States-inspired saboteurs and there was a major diplomatic incident.

British atomic tests were not exempt from UFO trouble. Three bombs were fired during September and October of 1957 at the Maralinga range in the Nullarbor Plain of Western Australia. Officer Derek Murray was sitting with his pals playing cards when an airman rushed in saying there was a UFO over the blast zone.

The RAF crew rushed out to see a metal disc surmounted by a dome hovering at a 45 degree angle. A row of windows was clearly visible. 'It was a magnificent sight,' Murray said later. There were no other aircraft in the vicinity at the time and the craft disappeared at a very high speed after a few moments.

ALIENS IN COLD STORAGE

The Roswell incident did not end with the revelations about the cover-up, which are now a matter of record. Rumours abounded for years afterwards that not only had wreckage been found, but that alien bodies had been recovered from other sites in the vicinity.

The stories were given credence by a civil engineer called Grady Barnett, who claimed to have stumbled upon another UFO crash site at the same time as the wreckage on Brazel's ranch was discovered. Barnett's crash site was 160 km/100 miles west of Roswell at Magdalena, near Socorro, New Mexico. He had been working for the Soil Conservation Service when he came upon a crashed disc.

Outside it were dead humanoid bodies. Barnett described themas being hairless, with large domed heads. He alleged that the site was also seen by a group of archaeology students who were working in the area.

All were hustled away by a group of military personnel who appeared on the scene shortly afterwards and took both the bodies and the wreckage. Some UFOlogists speculate that the wreckage found by Brazel at Roswell had broken off in mid-air from an alien spacecraft which managed to fly on to Magdalena before crashing. They believe the crash material and the remains were taken first to Hangar 18 at Wright Patterson airbase and shortly afterwards to Area 51 of the Tonopah airbase complex, 320 km/200 miles north of Las Vegas, where they remain to this day.

The truth or otherwise of Barnett's story has never been proved. He died in 1969, long before the facts about the cover-up at Roswell became widely known. Other UFO watchers suggest there may have been a third crash site no more than 4 km/2½ miles from the Roswell wreckage, and that four bodies had been found at the scene.

Whatever the case, Lieutenant Colonel Arthur Exon, who was serving at Wright Patterson airbase at that time, , later claimed to have spoken with base staff who had personally examined alien remains.

'They were all found in fairly good condition', he said, admitting that animals had got to the corpses before the air force and damaged some of the soft tissues.

Many people have since come forward with stories about 'extra-terrestrial biological entities', as the official designation was alleged to have been. The beings are commonly described as 1.20 metres to 1.50 metres (four to five feet) tall, humanoid with large heads and eyes and slit-like mouths.

Skull and bones seemed very fragile, according to one nurse who claimed to have taken part in an autopsy at Roswell before the material was transferred. One of the more convincing stories came from pilot Oliver Henderson, who claimed to have flown a spotter aircraft which found the bodies at Roswell.

He did not reveal this until 1982, after the first serious investigations by UFOlogists. Another man, Sergeant Melvin Brown, said he rode in a truck with the bodies from the crash site to Roswell airbase and stood guard over the hangar where they were stored.

Meanwhile, in what seems one of the most unlikely tales, an undertaker at Roswell remembers strange calls he received over the period regarding the preservation of soft tissue and the size of his smallest coffins. Secrecy still shrouded activities at the Wright Patterson airbase during the Forties and Fifties.

One woman, Norma Gardner, revealed after her retirement that she had catalogued UFO material while working there. She also claimed to have typed autopsy reports on the bodies of occupants and allegedly saw two of the bodies as they were being shipped to another site. More mysterious still is the memo from FBI field officer Guy Hottel to his boss, J Edgar Hoover, dated 22 March 1950 and thought to refer to yet another crash site – this time at Aztec, New Mexico.

Under the heading Flying Discs Or Flying Saucers it said: 'An investigator for the air force stated that three so-called flying saucers had been recovered in New Mexico. They were described as being circular in shape with raised centres, approximately 15 metres/50 feet in diameter.

There are very few photographs of alien entities, and no reliable ones. There have, however, been some very spectacular hoaxes, or suspected hoaxes. The photograph above allegedly depicts an alien taken alive from a UFO that crashed near Mexico City in the 1950s. There is no supportive evidence for this photograph

'Each one was dressed in metallic cloth of a very fine texture. The saucers were found in New Mexico due to the fact that the government has a very high-powered radar set-up in that area and it is believed the radar interferes with the controlling mechanism of the saucers'.

The memo was, quite unbelievably, marked 'no further evaluation' by FBI headquarters.

One fascinating tale is recounted by UFO writer Timothy Green Beckley, telling how a top electronics expert was flown to an airbase in New Jersey in the mid-1950s where he was shown a bizarre film and asked to 'analyse from the film anything he could define from his experience with radar technology'. The film showed a strange disc-shaped object with two guards, one on each side of the craft. The ship was sitting on two large blocks and the technician estimated it to be about 5.5 metres/18 feet in diameter. It was smooth on the outside, except for some tool marks around the entrance. A ramp extended from the ship to the ground.

After showing the inside of the craft, which looked bare apart from some simple control levers, the camera moved outside and focused on three small bodies with abnormally large heads which were laid out on a table.

The major in charge would only say that the craft and its occupants had been found in New Mexico.

Today, the official USAF line on Hangar 18 is that it does not exist. Its current designation is Building 18A, Area B. Surrounded by a high wire fence, its windows have all been knocked out and replaced with concrete.

As late as 1978, the UFOlogist Leonard Springfield claimed that he had reports and signed affidavits from 25 impeccable sources that spaceships and bodies were being held there.

In recent years, more attention has been focused upon Area 51 at Tonopah. It has been linked for years with the development of Stealth aircraft technology and, some suggest, with the even more advanced Aurora spy plane whose existence has still to be admitted officially.

Some UFOlogists believe Area 51 is home to at least nine alien spacecraft and the frozen corpses of their crew. Others go so far as to suggest the US government has identified the aliens as coming from the Zeta Reticuli star system. The Tonopah area is renowned for UFO sightings.

The mystery has deepened in recent years as federal authorities continue to buy up land around the base: more than 1620 hectares/4000 acres to date. Television crews and newspaper reporters are still repeatedly turned away from the perimeter and have their film confiscated.

The mystery surrounding Area 51, Hangar 18 and Roswell deepened still further in early 1995, when it was reported that a major US television company had acquired the rights to a 90-minute film taken at one of the Roswell crash sites. Allegedly, the footage was copied from official film in the late 1940s by an air force photographer.

It purports to show cranes lifting wreckage at the site and the face of then-President Harry S Truman is seen among the bystanders.

Whether or not the film proves authentic, the likelihood is that the mystery of what happened at Roswell may never be solved.

MEETING MR SPACEMAN

The Space Race caught the public's imagination on both sides of the Iron Curtain, and it was not long before some began to wonder whether the astronauts and cosmonauts might be seeing more than they were letting on.

They were encouraged in their beliefs by the cryptic words of rocket pioneer Dr Wernher von Braun, who in 1959 was interviewed after a Juno II rocket went off course while under test. Von Braun told the reporter: 'We find ourselves faced by powers which are far stronger than we had hitherto assumed, and whose base of operations is at present unknown to us. More I cannot say at present. We are now engaged in entering into closer contact with these powers and in six or nine months' time it may be possible to speak with more precision on the matter'.

USAF pilot Joe Walker revealed in May 1962 that he had photographed five or six UFOs while flying his X-15 experimental rocket plane at the very edge of space. He described the objects as disc-shaped and told Le Matin of Paris that part of his job was to detect UFOs.

Two months later another X-15 pilot, Major Robert White, offered more 'proof' to those who believed UFOs were in some way monitoring the space programme. 'There are things out there,' he radioed back from his cockpit. 'There absolutely are!'

What he had seen was a small unidentified blob and some flaky white material which may have been ice crystals breaking off his aircraft.

The United States' first astronaut, John Glenn, who had gone into orbit on 20 February 1962, confirmed the difficulties involved in identifying unknown objects outside the earth's atmosphere. Attempting to describe the view from his capsule, he said: 'A lot of the little things I thought were stars were actually a bright yellowish green and about the same size and intensity as looking at a firefly on a really dark night. There were literally thousands of them'.

Russian cosmonauts reported the same phenomenon, created by light bouncing off dust particles. Nevertheless there were those who still believed spacemen had seen other craft while in orbit.

Why did Voshkod I, for example, return to Earth after only a day in orbit in 1964 despite protests from the three-man crew? UFOlogists were quick to seize on the mystery, suggesting it may have been forced down by alien spacecraft. There was never the slightest evidence to support this.

In December the same year, the launch of Mariner IV from Cape Kennedy triggered a host of reports of cigar-shaped objects seen in the sky around the launch site and in the Miami area.

Numerous examples of strange blobs appearing in NASA pictures taken from satellites and manned spacecraft have since been reported. Most of them have been dismissed — sunlight bouncing off a bolt, lens flare, and so on. Only one case seems to defy explanation: that of Gemini 4.

Astronaut James McDivitt was passing over Hawaii on 4 June 1965 when he photographed a can-shaped UFO. When the prints were developed, the photo showed not a can shape but two blurred lights.

NASA was so concerned that it set up its own scientific study to examine the pictures. Probably they were more concerned that it might be a new Russian device than about flying saucers. The study failed to reach a conclusion, stating only that the pictures were 'a challenge to the analyst'. McDivitt insists the object was not debris from his own spacecraft.

There have also been some rather curious radio exchanges between mission control and American spacecraft over the years. On Gemini 7's mission, for instance, astronauts Borman and Lovell radioed:

'We have a bogey at 10 o'clock high'.

'Is that the booster or is that an actual sighting?'

'We have several . . . looks like debris up here . . . actual sighting'. The debris was described as 'tiny lights'. Lovell later said he had seen nothing in space which he could not explain.

UFOs over Paris photographed in 1953 (top)   Photograph taken at Plymouth Zoo, Devon in 1972 (bottom)

Few astronauts will discuss the subject of UFOs these days. However, one of the pioneers of the early Mercury flights created a storm when he addressed the UN on the subject in 1978.

'There are several of us who do believe in UFOs and have had occasion to see a UFO on the ground or from an airplane,' said Gordon Cooper. He also pointed out that astronauts were reluctant to discuss their experiences because of the 'great numbers of people who have indiscriminately sold fake stories and fraudulent documents abusing their names and reputations'.

Perhaps the most bizarre story put about by the wilder fringe of UFOlogists is the theory that the Apollo space missions were abandoned because aliens warned the Americans off. Aldrin and Armstrong are alleged to have seen some UFOs in a crater and Aldrin filmed them as Armstrong got out. His censored words are supposed to have run: 'These babies are huge, sir . . . enormous . . . I'm telling you there are other spacecraft out there'.

The story would be entirely laughable, had it not come from former NASA officials Otto Binder and Maurice Chatelain, former boss of the organisation's communications systems.

Another unattributed report had Armstrong telling an unnamed friend in military intelligence: 'We were warned off. There was never any question of a space station or a moon city'.

Armstrong and Aldrin: allegedly saw UFO on moon

Diehard UFOlogists will still tell you about the alien spacecraft that buzzed the space shuttle *Discovery* in 1989. But most experts now accept that whole thing was a clever hoax, even if it did make headlines all over the world.

The claim is that the crew of mission STS-29 sighted an alien spacecraft which somehow locked itself on to the shuttle, temporarily draining it of power. UFO investigator Donald Ratsch from Maryland had been monitoring shuttle radio traffic via the Goddard Amateur Radio Club. At 6.35am on 14 March 1989, he heard the words: 'We have a problem – we have a fire (some UFOlogists later claimed that 'fire' was a NASA code word for a UFO)'.

Seven minutes later came the message: 'Houston: *Discovery* . . . we still have the alien spacecraft under observation'.

The exchange was taped by Ratsch. Whether the voice was that of mission commander Michael Coats or pilot John Blaha is not clear; the tape sounds as if it is Blaha but he later denied that they were his words.

MUFON, the North American UFO group which Ratsch was working for, demanded full access to the mission's radio transcripts under the Freedom of Information Act.

NASA's public relations people replied that they did not produce written transcripts, but that audio tapes could be bought for a few hundred dollars. There were no photographs because there had been no sighting.

Their spokesperson Bunda Dean added: 'We believe that this is a fictitious event and is a hoax perpetrated by a rogue radio operator or an unlicensed person using radio equipment and broadcasting on a repeater frequency that some ham groups use to relay NASA transmissions'.

MUFON meanwhile attempted to use voice analysis on the tape. But the alleged message was too short to make any comparison. Eventually they agreed there was no firm evidence to support a positive sighting.

Mission Commander Coats spoke for the crew in May 1989: 'The reason why you will never hear an actual tape recording of any of us on *Discovery* discussing aliens is because we never did. The stories are amusing but pure fiction.

'If we did see any aliens, the whole world would hear about it immediately. We are just as curious about the possibility of other life as anyone, so why would we try to be secretive?'

AN AWFUL LOTTA UFOs
IN BRAZIL

South America has proved a magnet for Unidentified Fying Objects since the late 1940s. In particular, Brazil has provided evidence for some of the most extraordinary sightings and face-to-face encounters yet recorded. UFOlogists from all over the world continue to descend in particular on the Sao Jose region north of Sao Paulo. This is said to be the home of 'mother of gold': strange lights which are said to haunt the mountains by night.

Brazil continues to report more alien abductions than any other country — and indeed the sensational encounter of farmer Antonio Villas Boas was the first such case in modern times.

There have been numerous other episodes. Among them is what appears to be the first recorded UFO attack on humans. It took place on 4 November 1957 at a heavily-defended fort near Santos on the coast of Brazil.

Two sentries were on duty at around 2 am when they saw a bright light high in the sky above them, which they took to be an exploding star. Moments later, they realised that the light was descending on their position at a high speed. As it reached 300 metres/1000 feet, it slowed before descending to about 45 metres/150 feet.

The terrified soldiers could see now that the object was circular with a diameter roughly the wingspan of a DC-3 aircraft. It was bathed in a strange orange glow and it illuminated the ground and the nearby gun positions.

There was a strange buzzing noise and the men felt a wave of heat pass over them. One collapsed immediately, the other fled into the gun emplacements.

As he shouted for help, the lights in the fortress suddenly went out. Other soldiers rushed to the men's rescue in pitch darkness. It was a scene of total chaos. When the emergency generator was switched on, it lasted only a moment before cutting out.

At least two other troops saw the UFO, which had turned and headed out to sea. The two sentries were treated for second-degree and third-degree burns.

The mystery of what happened that night remains, despite attempts by Brazilian authorities to explain it. Whether the sentries had been victims of some sort of deliberately aimed heat ray or had simply been too close to the UFO's propulsion system will never be known.

A few months later, the Brazilian military was once again dumbstruck by a UFO sighting which was witnessed by 48 people who all signed statements to that effect. What is more, the object was captured on film. It was 16 January 1958 and the marine research vessel Almirante Saldanha was preparing to leave the tiny island of Trinidad in the South Atlantic. There were at least 300 people on board, including numerous highly-qualified marine researchers, geologists and scientists, and an expert in underwater photography called Almiro Barauna.

At around noon, the photographer armed with his Rolleiflex was preparing to shoot the scenes as the ship-to-shore transport pinnace was being hoisted aboard before departure. Suddenly, there was a great commotion and several people began pointing at a bright object which appeared to be flying towards the island. They shouted at Barauna, urging him to take photographs.

He managed to shoot six in 15 seconds before the object vanished from sight. The first two caught the UFO on its way in, the third as it emerged from behind a mountain, then there were two misses, and a sixth taken as the object sped into the distance.

The photographs taken that day are said by UFOlogists to be among the most convincing that have been taken anywhere in the world, not least because of the prudent steps taken by skipper Captain Carlos

Alberto Bacellar. He insisted the film was developed immediately in a washroom on board. The photographer was ordered to strip to his swimming trunks before starting work so he could not conceal any equipment used for doctoring the prints. The developing process was observed by a retired air force captain, Jose Theobaldo Viegos, and the still-wet negatives were inspected by Captain Bacellar, who matched the scenery around the vessel against them.

The pictures were later pronounced genuine by the Brazilian Navy and presented to the world by the country's president Juscelino Kubitschek. They show a metallic-looking globe with a central ring around it. Subsequent analysis suggests the object was travelling at a minimum 1200 km/750 miles per hour.

It was later revealed that there had been eight sightings in the area since the previous November, four of them over Trinidad within the previous 40 days.

As in other close encounters, the ship's electrical system blacked out as the UFO approached.

Shortly after the photographs were made public, the country's Navy Minister, Admiral Alves Camera, told reporters: 'The Brazilian Navy is involved in an important secret which cannot be made public, since there is no explanation for it. I have not believed in flying saucers until now, but Barauna's photographic proof has now convinced me'.

The last word on the Barauna pictures goes to Naval Commander Moreira da Silva, who said: 'I can in any case verify that the photos are authentic and that the film was developed on board the Almirante Saldanha; moreover that the negative was immediately examined by a number of different officers. Any possibility of a photographic forgery was completely excluded'.

A more sinister episode was recorded by police in Rio de Janeiro in August 1966 following the discovery of two bodies, both male. Police had been alerted by a call from a woman who said a UFO had landed on a hillside near the suburb of Niteroi. Near the summit, they encountered the victims, both of them wearing lead masks.

A note was found with the bodies which read: 'At 4.30 pm we will take the capsule. After the effect is produced, protect half the face with lead masks. Wait for the agreed signal'.

Neither of the men was ever identified (not an unusual state of affairs in the barrios of Rio). Forensic and pathology reports could give no indication as to the cause of death but several possibilities were ruled out, including poison, asphyxia and foul play. Had they been attempting to contact alien beings or simply victims of a killer who knew how to cover his tracks? The case has never been solved.

THE EUROPEAN EXPERIENCE

Much literature on the UFO phenomenon is dominated by the famous North American sightings, yet thousands of Europeans — and Britons in particular — have been witness to sensational encounters which continue to baffle seasoned investigators.

UFO incidents over European airports are particularly common. Manchester's Ringway and London's Heathrow and Gatwick are notorious. In January 1995, for instance, a British Airways 737 approaching Manchester's Ringway airport was buzzed by a fast-moving UFO, which hurtled directly towards them before veering off downside of the aircraft. The pilot instinctively dived before calling air traffic control, who told Captain Roger Wills and first officer Mark Stuart that there were no other aircraft in the area. A report detailing the crew's evidence was forwarded to the Civil Aviation Authority for investigation.

Unidentified flying objects had, of course, been common in central Europe and Scandinavia during the Second World War. Among them were the famous Foo Fighters which buzzed Allied bombers over Germany in the closing stages.

In the summer of 1946 there were numerous reports of 'ghost rockets' in the skies over Sweden and Greece. The Swedish government was so concerned that it set up a special investigation body.

Photographic evidence of UFOs in Europe did not come until 5 June 1955. A postman and amateur photographer called Muyldermans took several shots of a flying disc over the town of Namur, Belgium. Expert analysis suggests the object was around 1525 metres/5000 feet up and approximately 12 metres/40 feet in diameter.

In 1964 a Finnish sighting resulted in the recovery of material thought to have been jettisoned from a UFO. The craft was seen hovering over Kallavesi Lake near Kuopio by Raimo Blomqvist, who saw a small chunk of material fall from it into the water's edge just before speeding off.

The material was analysed and found to contain iron oxide and various trace elements. Experts at Akademi University X-rayed the material and stated that it was not a geological specimen, although its composition did resemble that of rock found near some volcanic sites. The possibility that it might be a meteorite was also ruled out. In short, the verdict was inconclusive.

The year 1967 saw a flurry of UFO activity in Britain, with the famous Moigne Downs encounter in Dorset proving to be one of the most significant. It is noteworthy largely because of the credibility of the chief witness, Angus Brooks, a former RAF intelligence officer.

Brooks had been walking his dogs on the morning of 26 October when a gale blew up. He took shelter by lying on his back in a slight shallow in the side of a hill and relaxed while the dogs ran about.

High in the sky, he spotted what appeared to be the vapour trail of a jet. A few moments later he realised that it was in fact a craft rushing headlong at him. It was a disc-shaped craft with long girder-like fuselages extending behind it. The machine came to a sudden halt some 370 metres/130 feet away, hovering 60 metres/200 feet off the ground. It was approximately 53 metres/175 feet in diameter, made of some sort of translucent metal. Brooks observed it for 22 minutes before it took off again.

Denmark had one of its most intriguing sightings on the night of 13 August 1973 when policeman Evald Maarup was driving home along a quiet country road. He suddenly found his vehicle bathed in brilliant white light. Both the car engine and his radio transmitter cut out instantaneously.

Maarup watched as the beam of light appeared to be sucked back into a large grey craft directly over-head. After five minutes, it sped off and the car and radio returned to normal. Colleagues initially ridiculed Maarup, suggesting he go to a mental hospital, but were eventually persuaded that he had seen something. The story broke and all hell broke loose. The Danish air force suggested that what the officer had seen was a jet trainer which had been in the area before. Maarup insisted on the truth of what he said he had seen.

One of the most celebrated encounters of the 1970s took place over the Atlantic Ocean about 40 miles south of Lisbon. Officers on the flight deck of a British Airways Trident overheard this conversation between Lisbon air traffic control and a TriStar flying above the BA aircraft:

'We have reports of the UFO. Could you confirm the sighting?'

The TriStar replied: 'Yes, we have this UFO in sight'.

At that point the crew of the Trident spotted a bright light in the distance and confirmed that they too could see the object, now joined by a long brown cigar shape slightly to its right.

The Trident captain radioed Lisbon: 'There is no way that this is a star or planet'. He then took the unusual step of informing passengers: 'If you look on the starboard side, you will see what we believe to be a UFO'.

The sighting was confirmed by a third aircraft, this time a TAP 727, and was witnessed by dozens of passengers, some of whom viewed it through binoculars.

The Trident landed, picked up more passengers and headed back towards London. The pilot made a point of checking the area where the UFO had been seen earlier and was amazed to find a massive radar return. The blip was so large that it would have been around 600,000 tonnes — three times the size of a supertanker. Despite turning down all the cabin lights, the crew could not make visual contact.

Italy has seen numerous reports of UFOs. One of the best-known took place at the Aviano NATO base in 1977. American soldier James Black saw a very bright object hovering over two military aircraft at the base. It was more than 30 metres/100 feet wide and was continually changing from red to green. On top there was a spinning dome of some sort.

The object remained on the spot for a hour and apparently blacked out the electricity supply to the base. The lights flashed back on as soon as the craft lifted off and headed beyond the horizon.

The official explanation was that it must have been moonlight reflected on the clouds.

European sightings continue to this day. One of the hottest spots for budding UFOlogists is the island of Gran Canaria which has a long history of sightings. But there have also been numerous sightings and alleged abductions in Sweden, Finland, Poland and Denmark.

MAGIC OR IMAGININGS?

Some stories of alien encounters have been so fantastically detailed that they have become woven into the fabric of UFOlogy and are quoted whenever a fresh study of the subject is made, a documentary is screened or a book is written. No apologies, then, for including two of the most famous of these cases in this volume, however outlandishly unlikely they appear. What they may teach us is that, however well-meaning, self-publicity is not the same thing as scientific acknowledgment. Indeed, it has often been said by the naturally sceptical that imagination is no substitute for evidence.

George Adamski was an amateur astronomer who lived near the Mount Palomar Hale observatory in California. On 20 November 1952 he and six friends drove deep into the Californian desert where they believed they had a better chance of seeing and photographing unidentified flying objects which had been reported in the area. Adamski, a Polish-born United States citizen who was then aged 61, claimed that their curiosity was rewarded by the sight of a fat cigar-shaped ship floating in the sky.

Adamski, who was enjoying a picnic with his friends when the sighting occurred, got a member of the party to drive him closer to a spot where he believed a craft might land. Speaking later on behalf of the group, he later said they believed that the cigar-shaped vessel was a mother ship and that any smaller craft which might land on Earth would come from its belly.

For some reason, Adamski persuaded his friends to leave him with cameras and a telescope, arguing that, alone, he had more chance of getting photographic evidence than if they were all together in a pack.

Adamski claimed that he did indeed see a flying saucer come from the mother ship, circle overhead, then drop out of sight. He had concluded that it must have returned to the command vessel when he spotted a man standing at the entrance to a ravine some distance away. Thinking the person could be in trouble alone in the desert, he made tracks towards him – and encountered, he said, a Venusian space traveller.

Adamski later wrote: 'Suddenly, as though a veil were removed from my mind, the feeling of caution left me so completely that I was no longer aware of my friends or whether they were observing me as they had been told to do. By this time we were quite close. He took four steps towards me, bringing us within arm's length of each other. Now, for the first time, I fully realised that I was in the presence of a man from space — a human being from another world'.

He reckoned the creature to be about 170 cm/5 feet 6 inches in height, of human form, aged about 28 in human terms, with a high forehead, large grey-green eyes, high cheekbones and fine white teeth which flashed when he smiled.

Communication was difficult as the spaceman spoke no English. Nevertheless, using sign language and what Adamski described as 'primitive telepathy', the duo made themselves understood up to a point. Adamski said the visitor was concerned about the Earth's radiation and its nuclear weapons, which were disturbing the balance of the universe.

As they talked, the Venusian gestured to the mother ship, indicating that it was time for the discussion to end and for him to leave. Adamski said he gave the Venusian a photographic plate of his craft, which he had taken when left alone by his friends. After promising to return, the spaceman departed and Adamski rejoined his companions.

What made Adamski's account seem somewhat plausible at the time was the fact that it was witnessed by his friends, who later signed sworn statements that they saw Adamski in conversation with the extra-terrestrial, and that they witnessed both his flying saucer and the mother ship.

However, Adamski's plausibility began to diminish when he went on to make a series of other very unlikely claims. According to the amateur astronomer, he continued to have many more fantastic adventures with spacemen, claiming to have met two emissaries of Mars and Saturn at a Los Angeles hotel and

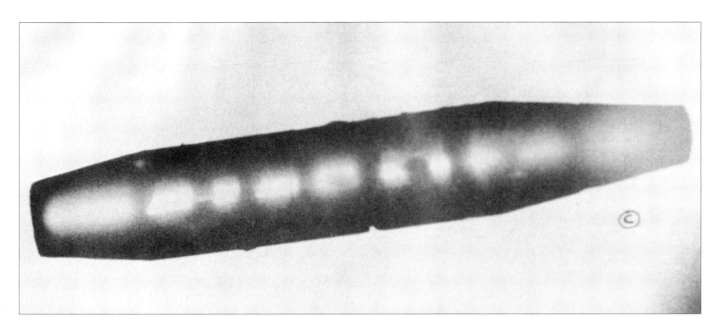

UFOs photographed by contactee George Adamski (top and bottom)

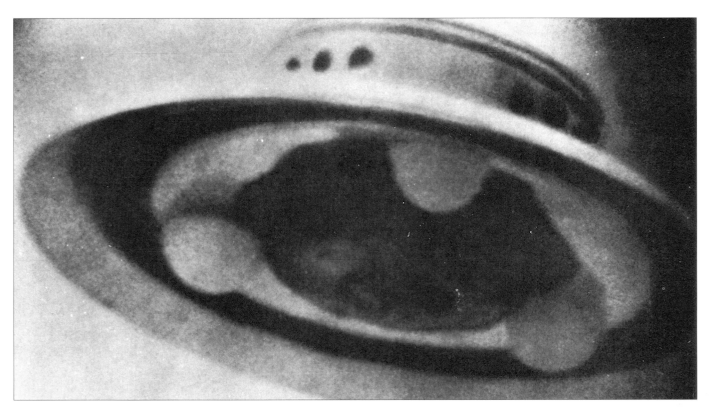

UFOs photographed by contactee George Adamski (top)   Spaceship Billy Meier claimed landed on his farm (bottom)

to have visited the moon, finding it to possess a lush area of vegetation and animals.

It was his later tall tales that discredited him — but he did produce a description of space that was almost mirrored by those of John Glenn and the other early astronauts.

A Swiss farmer named Billy Meier took up where George Adamski left off. For years he claimed to be the link on our planet with a space-race called Pleiadeans, inhabitants of the star cluster Pleiades, who allegedly closely resemble humans, but are of much higher intelligence.

Meier came to the attention of UFO researcher Wendelle Stevens, a retired USAF colonel from Tucson, Arizona, who has assembled a collection of some of the most intriguing UFO pictures ever taken. He began corresponding with Meier at his hill farm near Hinwell, in the Zurich canton, and was ecstatic about the pictures of flying saucers which the farmer sent to him.

Meier claimed to have made contact with the Pleiadeans in 1975, when they landed near his farm. There were three of them: Semjase, Ptaah and Asket. They said that before they had settled on Erra, a small planet in the Pleiades cluster, they had lived on a planet in the star constellation of Lyra, which had been torn apart in a thermo-nuclear war with rivals from other worlds.

They explained to him that Pleiadeans were 3000 times more advanced than humans and that their mission in coming to see him was to form a bond with Earth. Meier said that Semjase, who was a female Pleiadean, told him:

'We too are still far removed from perfection, and have to evolve constantly, just like yourselves. We are neither superior nor superhuman, nor are we missionaries. We feel duty bound to the citizens of Earth, because our forefathers were your forefathers. We have taken on certain tasks such as the supervision of developing life in space, particularly human, and to ensure a certain measure of order. In the course of these duties we approach the denizens of various worlds, select some individuals and instruct them. This we do only when a race is in a stage of higher evolution. Then we explain (and prove to them) that they are not the only thinking beings in the universe'.

Wendelle Stevens met Meier, and was captivated by him and his stories of his experiences with the Pleiadeans. In 1979 he published a book about Meier, in which he recorded and illustrated all of the UFO sightings, the Pleiadean philosophy — plus details of a flight which Meier claimed to have taken in a Pleiadean spacecraft.

The truth or otherwise of Meier's claims continues to arouse great passions — not least because of his later statements which, rather like Adamski's before him, became increasingly far-fetched as time progressed. Meier got his biggest headlines of all when he claimed that the space visitors took him on a time-and-space journey back to the ages of Jesus Christ and of the dinosaurs.

Yet the Swiss hill farmer still has disciples who argue that there is no reason why space travellers should not make contact with a humble toiler of the soil rather than a president or a king.

ANCIENT ENCOUNTERS

Encounters Of The Second Kind

'A UFO leaves its mark, causes burns or paralysis to humans, frightens animals, interferes with car engines or TV and radio reception, leaves landing marks'
– Dr J Allen Hynek, Centre For UFO Studies, Evanston, Illinois

ANCIENT VISITATIONS

Strange objects in the sky have mystified man since pre-history. Tales of visitations — even abductions — by 'forces unknown' have been around since the Stone Age. Therefore it is not surprising that, with more than 100,000 million stars in our galaxy alone, reports of alien encounters have topped the tens of thousand since man first learned to write.

Many believe that we have been visited by intelligent life forms from the depths of space since time began. The following chapters report on some of the earliest phenomena — from the 'spaceship landing grounds' of South America to the 'tribal astronomers' of Africa.

One of the earliest written reports of a UFO is in the ancient Indian text Samarangana Sartradhara, which dates back to 500 BC It contains descriptions of strange, piloted flying machines called 'vimanas' with unexplained power sources. The same vimanas are described in various Sanskrit texts — adding that such was their power and range that they could 'carry death' anywhere on planet Earth.

A sighting at Hadria in Italy in 214 BC was described two centuries later by the Roman writer Livy, who said it looked like 'an altar in the sky'. Historian Pliny the Elder reported on a giant 'spark as big as a moon' that fell from the sky in AD 66, then returned into the heavens. In his Historia Naturalis, Pliny wrote of 'a light from the sky by night, a phenomenon usually called "night suns", [which] was seen often, causing apparent daylight in the night'. On another occasion 'a burning shield scattering sparks ran across the sky at sunset from east to west'.

Mediaeval literature abounds in UFO reports. The bishop of Tours, France, wrote in his Historia Francorum in AD 584-85 of how 'there appeared in the sky brilliant rays of light', how 'signs, that is to say rays and domes such as are customarily seen, race across the sky' and how 'golden globes' made their heavenly appearances.

Many early UFO sightings were explained away as being visits by 'dragons,' this perhaps being the only way our unscientific ancestors could come to terms with strange glowing objects in the sky. The Anglo-Saxon Chronicles, written in AD 793, tell this graphic tale: 'In this year terrible portents appeared in Northumbria and miserably afflicted the inhabitants. These were exceptional flashing of lightning and fiery dragons seen flying through the air'.

Another English chronicler, Ralph Niger, told how a 'wonderfully large dragon' was seen at St Osyth, Essex, in 1170. This dragon was 'borne up from the earth through the air. The air was kindled into fire by its motion and burned a house, reducing it and its outbuildings to ashes'.

On New Year's Day 1254, monks at St Albans, Hertfordshire, sighted 'a kind of ship, large, elegantly-shaped and well-equipped, and of a marvellous colour'. In 1290 monks at Byland Abbey, Yorkshire, saw 'a large, round, silver disc' passing overhead.

One of the most spectacular UFO display of all time occurred above the German city of Nuremberg on 4 April 1561. In what a citizen of the time described as 'a very frightful spectacle', glowing tubes, globes and crosses appeared in the sky in broad daylight and appeared to do battle for an hour before falling to earth 'as if on fire'.

A similar spectacle occurred over Basle, Switzerland, on 7 August 1566. Contemporary prints graphically portray giant glowing discs covering the sky. About two centuries later, in 1762, two Basle astronomers observed a 'spindle-like object' with a glowing umbra pass in front of the sun.

One of the earliest reliably recorded cases of an actual abduction was unearthed by astronomer Carl Sagan. The date was 1645 and the victim was a Cornish teenager named Anne Jeffries. Sagan says: 'Anne was found on the floor. Much later she recalled being attacked by little men, carried paralysed to a castle in the air, seduced and returned home. She called the little men "faeries". The next year she was arrested for witchcraft'.

A 'very frightful spectacle' was seen in the sky over Nuremberg at sunrise on 14 April 1561. Illustration taken from the Nuremberg Broadsheet, 1561

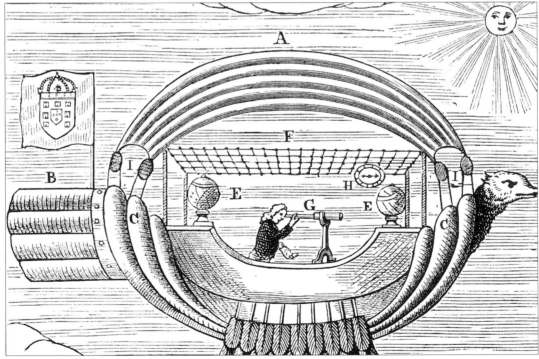

Large black globes were seen over Basel in August 1566 (top)   Flying ship as described in the Evening Post *in 1709 and allegedly invented by a Brazilian priest (bottom)*

ANCIENT VISITATIONS

Astronomy became a more sophisticated science in the 19th century, thereby increasing the number and quality of UFO records. A squadron of saucer-shaped objects was seen over the French town of Embrun in 1820 — changing course by 90 degrees without for a moment breaking formation. London's Greenwich Royal Observatory recorded a huge disc, illuminated by moonlight, which turned into a cigar-shaped object as it traversed the heavens. It is what we have come to know as a classic UFO sighting.

The term 'flying saucer' was not to be used for more than half a century, but in 1878 rancher John Martin described an object over the Texas town of Denison as being 'about the shape of a large saucer'.

Probably the first photograph of a UFO was taken through a telescope at Zacatecas observatory, Mexico in 1883. It followed a rash of sightings throughout the country in the 1880s.

The years 1896 and 1897 saw an astonishing outbreak of UFOs in North America. During November 1896 reports flooded in from all parts of California — a typical description from Sacramento being of a cigar-shaped craft floating sedately through the skies, with a bright light just below it. The following year hundreds of similar sightings were recorded in the Great Lakes states and later in Texas. Most spoke of elliptical objects which we would now consider to be like airships or dirigibles. Yet airships on this scale were not built until 1900 — and even then only in Germany.

In Kansas City, Missouri in 1897, an estimated 10,000 people witnessed a fascinating air display over the city – one of the largest audiences known for a UFO sighting. Psychic researcher Charles Fort wrote: 'Object appeared very swiftly then appeared to stop and hover over the city for ten minutes at a time. Then, after flashing green, blue and white lights, it shot upwards into space'.

In that same month, April 1897, Alexander Hamilton, a member of the House of Representatives, had an encounter of the closest kind with aliens at his farm in Le Roy, Kansas. In a sworn statement, he said he witnessed the landing of 'a cigar-shaped craft, about 300 feet long' with a carriage underneath. He added: 'The carriage was made of glass or some other transparent substance, alternating with a narrow strip of material. It was brilliantly lighted and everything within was clearly visible. It was occupied by six of the strangest beings I ever saw. They were jabbering together but I could not understand a word they said'.

Hamilton said that he and two of his farm hands tried to get near to the strange craft, but the aliens switched on some unknown power source and the UFO soared into the sky.

The age of the aircraft had not yet dawned. It would not be for another six years that Orville Wright first flew a 'heavier than air machine' at Kitty Hawk, North Carolina, in 1903. And yet, as we have seen, faithfully recorded sightings of aerial craft have occurred for hundreds, indeed thousands, of years.

Certainly the incidence of UFO sightings has increased in recent years. But the notion that they are a phenomenon of our modern age is arrogantly false. In fact, it looks as if our visitors from space have been paying their respects to Earth for longer than we have been around to witness them.

Even royalty was treated to UFO displays. In 1783, the court was gathered for a celebration by King George III and Queen Charlotte of the birth of their 15th child. On the fine summer's evening of 8 August, the gentry were sunning themselves on one of the terraces of the royal residence when they were privileged to observe an Unidentified Flying Object performing aerobatics over the River Thames valley stretched out beneath them. One of their number, the scientist Tiberius Cavallo, wrote this account of the incident:

'We suddenly saw appear an oblong cloud moving more or less parallel to the horizon. Under this cloud could be seen a luminous object which soon became spherical, brilliantly lit, and which came to a halt. This strange sphere seemed at first to be pale blue in colour, but its luminosity increased and soon it set off again towards the east. Then the object changed direction and moved parallel to the horizon before disappearing to the south-east. The light it gave out was prodigious; it lit up everything on the ground. Before it vanished it changed its shape, became oblong, and at the same time as a sort of trail appeared, it seemed to separate into two small bodies. Scarcely two minutes later the sound of an explosion was heard'.

THE ROBOZERO RIDDLE

It was not until political relations between the Soviet Union and the West began to improve that the Soviets admitted that the phenomenon of UFOs had been reported in their territory. For years the Soviet authorities had been anxious to play down reports of sightings because they believed the mysterious and exciting accounts would only arouse fear in their people.

But there was one mysterious happening which Soviet scientists — and their imperial counterparts before them — had studied for decades and which even today has no logical explanation. It is the Robozero Riddle, an event which occurred in 1663 and is one of the best-chronicled early sightings of a UFO. Attempts over the years to prove exactly what it was have come to nothing, and the mystery of what happened in the skies above a small Soviet community still provokes enormous debate within that area – and indeed, beyond.

The following account was submitted by a minor government official to the priests of a monastery near Robozero, a village 650 kilometres from St Petersburg.

The account was believed by the priests at the monastery — and was submitted by a man who was aware that the price of incurring their disbelief and displeasure was high. The monks were virtually omnipotent and terrible in their punishment: if they had thought what he wrote was false, his head would have rolled.

The official, however, was only one of hundreds of people who witnessed the strange phenomenon. This was the account he sent: 'Most venerable lords, humble greetings from your servant Ivachko Rjesvkoi. The peasant Levka Fedorov, domiciled in the village of Mys, submitted to me the following first-hand account –

"On this, the fifteenth day of August in the year 1663, a Saturday, the faithful from the district of Belozero had gone to church in large numbers in the village of Robozero and whilst they were there a great crash sounded out of the heavens and many people left the church of God to assemble outside on the square.

"Around the stroke of midday there descended upon Robozero a great ball of fire from the clearest of skies, not from a cloud; moreover it came from the direction from which we get winter and moved across the church to the lake. The fire was about 150 feet on each side, and for the same distance in front of the fire there were two fiery beams.

"Suddenly it was no longer there but about one hour of the clock later it appeared again, above the lake from which it had disappeared before. It went from the south to the west and was about 1650 feet away when it vanished. But once again it returned, filling all who saw it with a great dread, travelling west-wards and staying over Robozero one hour and a half.

"Now there were fishermen in their boat on the lake about a mile away and they were sorely burnt by the fire. The lake water was lit up to its greatest depths of 30 feet and the fish fled to the banks. The water seemed to be covered with rust under the glow".'

The story of what happened to the God-fearing people of Robozero spread like wildfire throughout Imperial Russia. The writer, Rjesvkoi, was subjected to a rudimentary examination by doctors to prove that he was not mad. Other witnesses were called forward and the authorities were satisfied that the fire-ball which appeared was genuine; some 500 people in all had witnessed the event.

Traces of the rust deposit continued to lap the shores of the lake for weeks, and fishermen reported that their nets, months afterwards, were filled with fish which showed burn marks and a translucent quality, which made them appear as if they were held up to a bright sunlight.

Two groups, completely separate from each other, witnessed the incredible spectacle — one was in the church square, the other on the lakeside, several hundred metres away.

Robozero Riddle: best chronicled early sightings of a UFO in 1663

For many, the site at Robozero became a holy shrine. The people were convinced that the place had been visited by God, who was telling them that they should pay homage to him there. The scientists of the day could not put forward any plausible explanations. One of the earliest theories propounded was that the people who witnessed the phenomenon had somehow fallen victims of a mass hallucination. However, the evidence of the separate groups — and the very real burns suffered by the lake fishermen — debunked this hypothesis.

It was not until this century that serious scientific analysis was brought to bear on the Robozero Riddle. Apart from the UFO explanation, theories put forward included a meteor, a comet and ball lightning. All three explanations had huge flaws in them. None accorded with the eye-witness reports of the day.

An Australia radio-astronomer called Robert Bracewell announced his own startling theory at a lecture delivered in the Soviet city of Byurakan in 1971. He claimed that there are civilisations in the centre of the Milky Way which are able to send out probes in every direction to seek out new life on other planets.

He argued that the fireball above a small Russian community all those years ago was in fact a space probe seeking to make contact with Earth. The rust residue on the water was the result of spent fuel from the probe and the appearance, disappearance and reappearance all indicated the ability of the probe to come and go at will, unlike meteors or other natural phenomena.

The Russians were, naturally, taken aback by this theory, which was unorthodox to say the least. But an anonymous author in the Russian magazine *Science is Power* admitted that orthodox inquiries had still failed to answer the riddle of Robozero and declared:

'The solution to the Robozero riddle is not known to any mortal, but anybody can attempt to solve it. Does a solution exist? Whoever knows it let him speak . . . '

In 1915 Dimitri Sviatski, of Petrograd University, put forward the theory that Robozero had been hit by a meteor. He wrote in *Astronomical Phenomena* in *Russian Chronicles*: 'The explosion of the meteor on 15 August 1663 probably occurred in a south-westerly direction during the morning before 12 o'clock and in clear skies. Two fragments were projected in a southerly direction over the lake whilst a third and fourth came down in the west'.

Sviatski had previously studied the effects of the huge fireball which wiped out great tracts of land in Siberia's Tunguska region in 1908. But his explanation left many unanswered questions.

Did the statements of the peasants and fishermen not prove that it was one and the same object seen at different times? And as a rule do meteorites not shed their fragments simultaneously? Also, the witnesses were able to follow the path of the object through the sky, and during a ten-minute walk from the church to the lakeside it was still visible. There has never been a meteor that travelled so slowly as to allow people to stroll after it as it hovered in the sky for them to observe — since it is estimated that meteorites travel at around 50 km/31 miles per second.

Furthermore, an explosion of a meteor over Robozero would have had the same effect as the fireball had at Tunguska: total devastation.

Another theory, put forward ten years later by professors at Moscow University, was that the Robozero object may have been a comet which had slipped from its orbit. The heat burns and rust residue in the waters of the lake might be explicable as the detritus of the the object's tail. However, the academics agreed that a comet coming to Earth in this way was extremely unlikely, and calculated the chances of it happening as being only once in 80 million years.

Only one other theory — apart from the possibility of a UFO — has been put forward by Soviet academics as a possible answer to the Robozero Riddle: ball lightning. This phenomenon occurs mostly in summer months and travels at high speeds across the sky.

Soviet scientist R A Leonov, in his publication The Riddle Of Ball Lightning, published in 1965, asserts that ball lightning can attain speeds up to 100 km/62 miles an hour and has a red or orange flame. Its presence is usually preceded by ordinary lightning. However, the ancient record shows that the fireball came from a clear sky and not a cloudy one. The duration of the phenomenon is also inconsistent with ball lightning. And besides, it does not explain the rusty residue on the water of the lake or the burns suffered by the witnesses.

'GODS' FROM SPACE

The people of the Dogon tribe had detailed knowledge of stars and planets many hundreds of years before they were observed scientifically. How did they gain such knowledge without using telescopes, astronomical charts and advanced mathematical theory? Is there any other explanation than that they learned these secrets from extra-terrestrial beings — visitors from other parts of the galaxy?

The Dogons of West Africa live in a scattering of villages over a vast area of what is now the Republic of Mali. The terrain is rocky and arid, and their homes are built of mud and straw. By Western standards, their lifestyle is primitive in the extreme.

Our fascination with them and their mysterious past is due to their own peculiar fascination with one single star: Sirius. This glittering star, one of the brightest in the heavens – as seen from Earth – is the lynch-pin of the Dogons' life. Their culture, ornamentation and even their religion centre around it. Sirius has been their enduring cult, and it was their knowledge of this distant source of light that has bewitched and bewildered the scientists of today.

When anthropologists first seriously began to investigate the history of the Dogons, they found that they did not really belong to the region; they had migrated to West Africa and settled on the Bandiagra Plateau some time between the 13th and 16th centuries. They believed themselves to be more gifted than their neighbours, and the reason was the secrets that they brought with them from the East — secrets they could not have been expected to know, even with today's technology.

Two French anthropologists, Marcel Griaule and Germaine Dieterlen, lived among the Dogons in the 1930s, winning their confidence and studying their intricate social structure. As the visitors were let into the secrets of the community, they became increasingly amazed at the tribesmen's depth of knowledge of the universe.

The Dogons knew that the Earth was round. They had also deduced that our planet spun on a north-south axis as it revolved around the Sun. They described the Moon as 'dry and dead like dry dead blood.'

This was impressive enough in itself, but it was when the tribe began to map out the rest of the solar system that the French anthropologists really began to take interest. The Dogons drew charts on the earth floors of their huts showing a series of rings around Saturn. They showed four moons circling Jupiter. They drew the Milky Way in the shape of a spiral. Without sophisticated astronomical equipment, it is amazing that these facts could have been known.

The Dogons then divulged their knowledge and beliefs about the broader galaxy beyond our own Solar System. Their information, puzzling at first, was to shock Marcel Griaule and Germaine Dieterlen — and eventually the world of astronomy.

At the heart of the Dogon beliefs about the universe is the star Sirius, to them the most magical in the galaxy. They revered it in the same way as many other cultures, from the cavemen to the Druids, deified our own Sun. The Dogons religiously charted every star and planet that passed around and interacted with Sirius in the night sky.

One of Sirius's oddities is that it has a companion star, now known as Sirius B, which is completely invisible to the naked eye. Indeed, it is so outshone by its near neighbour that its very existence was not even suspected by astronomers until the 19th century. Any real clues to its nature were not revealed until the 1920s. And it was not captured on a photograph until 1970.

This is unsurprising, for Sirius B is 100,000 times less bright than Sirius itself. It is an infinitesimal speck dwarfed by all the stars around it in the night sky. Yet every detail of Sirius B was recorded by the Dogons — a people whose primitive existence offered no outward clue to the wealth of astronomical knowledge they have had for centuries.

'The Dogon not only knew about this star but many of its characteristics', says author Francis Hitching

ANCIENT VISITATIONS

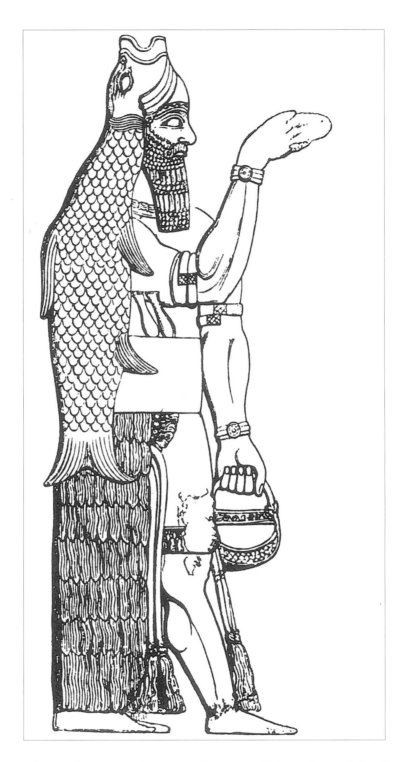

The curious Babylonian demigod Oannes who – according to tradition – descended to found civilisation on Earth

Famous stone statues on Easter Island that von Däniken suggests were erected by visitors from outer space

Carvings at the palace at Palenque. One stone relief, according to von Däniken, clearly depicts spacemen in helmets and he cites this as evidence supporting his theory that extra-terrestrials visited Earth in prehistory

in his World Atlas of Mysteries. 'He knew that it was white and although it was "the smallest thing there is" it was also "the heaviest star", made of a substance "heavier than all the iron on Earth". '

This, says Hitching, is a good description of Sirius B's density, which is so great that a single cubic metre weighs 20,000 tonnes. Dogon drawings also revealed the true orbit of Sirius B around Sirius: once every 50 years in an elliptical path.

The French anthropologists were astounded by these revelations which had been so unsensationally presented to them while squatting around the mud huts of a supposedly backward race. Griaule and Dieterlen wrote in one of their scientific reports: 'The problem of knowing how, with no instruments at their disposal, men could discern the movements and certain characteristics of virtually invisible stars has not been settled'.

After World War II, Marcel Griaule returned to Africa and was allowed by the Dogon priests to share their innermost secrets. Any discoveries he had by then made counted almost as nought compared with what he now learned. For the Dogons told him that they had been taught their extensive knowledge by visitors to Earth who came from a planet orbiting Sirius B.

In 1946 the scholar Robert Temple read all the reports on the Dogons by Griaule and Dieterlen; he then interviewed them in Paris and visited West Africa to pursue his research. His findings, as revealed in his book *The Sirius Mystery*, were that the Dogons worshipped alien creatures whom they called *Nommos* and who, according to their drawings, came to Earth in whirling spaceships or arks.

Dogon priests described these extra-terrestrial visitors as: 'The monitors of the universe, the fathers of mankind, guardians of its spiritual principles, dispensers of rain and masters of water.'

In *The Sirius Mystery*, Temple writes: 'The descriptions of the landing of the ark are extremely precise. The ark is said to have landed on the Earth to the north-east of the Dogon country, which is where the Dogon claim to have come from originally.

'The Dogon describe the sound of the landing of the ark. They say the "word" of Nommo was cast down by him in the four directions as he descended, and it sounded like the echoing of the four large stone blocks being struck with stones by the children, according to special rhythms, in a very small cave near Lake Debo. Presumably a thunderous vibrating sound is what the Dogon are trying to convey. One can imagine standing in the cave and holding one's ears at the noise. The descent of the ark must have sounded like a jet at close range'.

The ark's landing as it skidded to Earth 'displaced a pile of dust raised by the whirlwind it caused. The violence of the impact roughened the ground . . .'

Thus, according to the Dogons, the extra-terrestrials found their way to Earth — and to the chosen recipients of their superior knowledge.

What further evidence can be provided to support such seemingly wild claims? When the French anthropologists wrote their reports detailing the legends of the Dogons, they made a further claim that seemed to weaken rather than strengthen their case. They said there was a third star in orbit around Sirius — a third star influencing its movement in the heavens, although this new star was four times lighter in weight than Sirius B.

At the time of the French reports, there was no real evidence for a third star, a 'Sirius C'. But some astronomers later reported that they had indeed detected such a star, possibly a 'red dwarf', extremely difficult to detect.

London University scientists have produced a computer analysis of Sirius showing evidence for this third star, with an elliptical orbit taking up to four centuries to circle Sirius itself. This latest discovery is just as the Dogons foretold.

The scepticism that at first greeted the findings of Marcel Griaule and Germaine Dieterlen was almost as great as that which met the pronouncements of the most famous astronomer of all: Galileo. In 1610 the inventor of the telescope was accused of self-deception when he announced, among other things, that Jupiter had four main moons. Three and a half centuries later, there was a similar reaction when the Dogons made exactly the same pronouncement.

When Marcel Griaule and his partner published their learned papers, it was suggested that they had been misled by the Dogon priests. But there could be no doubt that Marcel Griaule had been told the truth. Having lived among the Dogons for 21 years, he was accepted as a tribal priest. in his own right. And when he died in 1956, about 250,000 people attended his funeral in Mali.

Author Robert Temple researched the Dogons' movements before their arrival in West Africa, believing justly that the tribe's history would provide clues to its seemingly limitless knowledge of astronomy. He discovered that the two million or more members of the Dogons and closely associated tribes had originated far from their present habitation. Their real homeland was inNorth Africa, probably in what is now Libya.

Until their migration, between 400 and 700 years ago, the tribe's closest cultural links would have been with the Egyptians, and before them the Babylonians and Greeks. Temple found that in both Greek and Babylonian mythology there are stories of beings from another world who had supernatural powers, and who passed on astronomical and astrological knowledge to Earthlings. In both cases, these alien creatures were amphibian and they helped to civilise this planet.

The story of the discovery of the dim star Sirius B is fascinating in itself. In the early 1800s astronomers realised that the principal star Sirius was acting strangely. Irregularities in the star's movements could only mean that it was being affected by another body, close to it in astronomical terms. Scientists decided that there must be another star with an enormous mass in the vicinity of Sirius which remained invisible to the human eye, however powerful a telescope was used.

It was not until the 1920s that a logical explanation was put forward. British scientist Sir Arthur Eddington suggested that some stars, when nearing the end of their lives, collapse in on themselves and take on a density out of proportion with their decreased size. Sirius B is such a star, which explained why such a relatively small object exerts a disproportionate gravitational force in the universe.

This scientific information has come to light in only recent times. Yet this theory and the existence of Sirius B were known about thousands of years ago by the Dogons.

SPACE MAPS

If we accept that it is likely that aliens have visited and continue to visit us, it is worth considering the theories of Swiss-born author Erich von Däniken, which put forward the idea that many of the Earth's ancient constructions may have been built to guide space travellers — or even been built *by* them.

In a series of books, von Däniken has suggested that mysterious constructions and prehistoric sites around the world are the result of ancient visitations by alien astronauts. Von Däniken's works have been much criticised and some of his findings disputed. Nevertheless, the questions he raises are challenging and largely unanswered.

The Nazca Desert, in the arid coastal plain of Peru in South America, is one possible site. Carved into the barren landscape are thousands of lines and figures — a giant humming-bird and a monkey are just two of them. The lines run in a geometric pattern and criss-cross each other, while the figures are etched between them.

The Nazca Lines have baffled scientists ever since American researcher Paul Kosok visited the site in 1940. What he found fascinated him. The lines are precisely drawn across the floor of the desert, some crossing mountains, some in perfect geometrical form, some plunging over cliffs. They were made by scraping the top surface of stones from the desert floor, leaving lighter soil showing beneath.

Kosok hired an aircraft to gain a clearer idea of the formation of the lines. It was only then that he realised he was examining work of an intelligence and an artistry far greater than he had believed could be possible. For, from the air, the lines not only made up geometrical forms like triangles and rectangles but also giant drawings of birds, fish and mammals.

One evening Kosok made the observation that a major line pointed directly to the setting sun on the day of the winter solstice. Because of this, he decided that Nazca was 'the largest astronomy book in the world'. He teamed up with German astronomer Maria Reiche to make a lifetime study of the lines. Although Kosok died in 1959, Reiche continued her study of the desert, coming up with a dozen theories but no answer to the enigma.

Various theories have been put forward to explain the Nazca phenomenon. The most scholarly of these is that the lines were constructed by the Nazca Indians as religious symbols 1500 years ago. Another idea is that they are the markings where canals and irrigation ditches were intended to be dug.

Erich von Däniken, however, proposed a far more startling theory: the markings are really mammoth landing strips, and that Nazca was an airfield used by extra-terrestrial beings thousands of years ago. This, he said, accounts for the straight lines in the desert.

By the time the spacemen eventually departed, the Nazca natives treated them as gods, claimed the author. Hoping for their return, the natives extended the airstrip with elaborate artistry as a means of enticing back the interplanetary voyagers.

Another mysterious place which, it has been suggested, spacemen may have constructed as a landing strip is in a remote mountainous area of Chile called El Enladrillado. It was not rediscovered until 1968. It is a plateau covered in 200 huge rectangular stone blocks from approximately 3.5 to 5 metres (11 ½ feet to 16½ feet) high and 6 to 9 metres (approximately 19½ to 29½ feet) long.

The stones have been grouped together, and at first glance the smooth, polished blocks look as though they form part of a massive amphitheatre. But even in recent years, the plateau, which is 3 kilometres (just under 2 miles) long, could be reached only by an arduous three-hour journey on horseback.

Who on earth could have constructed such a magnificent structure thousands of years ago? Humbert Bounaud, who led the 1968 expedition, said he believed the stones to have been the work of an ancient, unknown civilisation because the region's natives were incapable of such achievements. And, like von Däniken later, he also noted that part of the plateau would make an excellent landing site for flying

ANCIENT VISITATIONS

Von Däniken suggests these giant statues on Easter Island were created by marooned spacemen to attract help from their comrades in space

machines, the carefully hewn stones designed not as an amphitheatre at all, but as a giant landing strip for spacemen to home in on.

The vast stone statues of Easter Island in the Pacific also pose questions that von Däniken has tried to solve. How could such hard volcanic rock have been hewn, given the primitive tools found on the isle? How could such colossal monoliths have been moved across the terrain? And why do the statues depict men with thin lips, long noses and low foreheads when no islanders, past or present, have ever looked like that?

No-one has yet come up with a satisfactory explanation as to how the statues could have been made by primitive man. Von Däniken's answer is that space visitors, stranded on this planet after their craft had suffered some kind of breakdown, created the statues to attract help from their comrades in other ships. Some of the statues remain unfinished — proof, suggests von Däniken, that they were rescued before all the 'SOS' structures were completed.

Controversial theories such as these struck a strong chord with a fascinated public through von Däniken's books, Chariots Of The Gods and Return To The Stars. In them, the writer argued that 20th-century people should take the beliefs of ancient civilisations more literally. Most cultures, he pointed out, have legends of gods descending from the skies. Mankind is presently spending billions of pounds in the attempt to seek life in outer space, so why, he asked, deny the possibility of living 'gods' — creatures from space — having mastered space travel and having visited Earth in the past, prompting myth, legend and indeed religions?

Von Däniken has cited carvings from around the world as depicting spacemen in helmets, often with breathing apparatus. The most famous of these is the 'spaceman in a rocket ship' — the ancient stone relief discovered in the ancient site at Palenque, Mexico, in 1935. In Chariots of the Gods, the author described the carving in these words:

'There sits a human being, with the upper part of his body bent forward like a racing motorcyclist. Today any child would identify his vehicle as a rocket. It is pointed at the front, then changes to strange-ly grooved indentations like inlet ports, widens out and terminates at the tail in a darting flame. The crouching being himself is manipulating a number of undefinable controls and has the heel of his left foot on a kind of pedal. His clothing is appropriate: short trousers with a broad belt, a jacket with a modern Japanese opening at the neck and closely fitting bands at arms and legs'.

Von Däniken described the helmet as having 'the usual indentations and tubes, and something like antennae on top'. He concluded: 'Our space traveller — he is clearly depicted as one — is not only bent forward tensely, he is also looking intently at an apparatus hanging in front of his face'.

Von Däniken also attempted to explain the riddle of the lost city of Tiahuanaco in Bolivia. He said its huge stone arches, its statues of strange-looking men and its astonishingly accurate astronomical carv-ings all point to extra-terrestrial visitation. The Egyptian pyramids, Australian aboriginal rock paintings and the monoliths of Stonehenge are among many other phenomena in Erich von Däniken's catalogue of constructions supposedly created with the help of space visitors.

His theories have often been decried. Critics claim that he has conveniently used every mystery and riddle of the ancient world to bolster his argument that spacemen visited the earth centuries ago. Yet these ancient marvels still defy explanation by scholars. And it is too soon to write off the theory that man is not the only being to have walked on planet Earth.

Giant stone statues of the Pacific and vast maps marked on a Peruvian desert lack one vital element: a living human witness. So it is to this century that we must now look for the hundreds of thousands of well-documented alien sightings.

CLOSEST ENCOUNTERS

Encounters Of The Third Kind
'Humans see or meet UFOnauts'
– Dr J Allen Hynek, Centre For UFO Studies, Evanston, Illinois

THE LAVENDER FIELD ENCOUNTER

Thousands of people worldwide claim to have seen alien beings. Many have a history of mental illness, some are clearly charlatans or rogues. Others simply want to see their own face in the newspapers.

In recent years, a number of cases have hinged on the controversial — and now largely discredited — technique of 'regression analysis', which uses hypnosis to help subjects relive their encounter. But among all these are a handful of instances which remain both intriguing and inexplicable unless the words of the witness or witnesses are taken at face value. What is more, there are striking similarities between them.

One of the most famous of such encounters is that of farmer Maurice Masse on the morning of 1 July 1965 at Valensole, southern France. He had stopped in the shade for a quiet cigarette before continuing work in the lavender fields opposite when he heard a whirring noise above him. He walked out into the field expecting to catch a glimpse of a military helicopter. Instead, about a hundred yards from where he stood, was a curious egg-shaped object the size of a small car. It was supported on six spindly legs and had a raised dome on top of it. It stood about 2.5 metres/8 feet high.

In front of the machine were two figures, apparently examining plants in the field. On first sight, Masse suspected they were two small boys who had vandalised his crop the week before. However, looking more closely, he realised this was not the case.

The figures had large, bald heads, slanting eyes and lipless mouths. They appeared to have no necks, their heads and torso merging into each other at the shoulders. Both wore green boiler suits with a belt around the middle from which hung small metal cylinders.

As the farmer approached within 18 metres/60 yards of the beings, they turned and raised one of the cylinders at him. A beam of light struck and paralysed him.

He was able to watch as the beings entered their craft through a roller-blind type hatch and saw them looking back at him from the transparent dome of their craft. A moment later — still rooted to the spot — he saw them take off in their strange-looking craft. It took another 15 minutes for the paralysis to wear off. A startled Masse rushed home to tell friends what had happened.

'The strangers had such a calm and peaceful aura about them', he said later, 'that I was not in the least bit afraid'.

Subsequent investigations of the area revealed a higher-than-normal calcium content in the soil around the landing site. Lavender planted there afterwards withered and died, until the field was ploughed and the earth turned over.

Valensole was not the first instance of a close encounter on French soil. Ten years earlier there had been a mysterious incident at Quarouble.

On the night of 10 September 1954, Marius Dewilde was woken by his dogs howling. He opened his front door to find two glass-helmeted figures in one-piece suits standing a few feet from him. Dewilde rushed towards them in an attempt to grab one but was paralysed by a beam of light from a craft resting on the nearby railway track. A few moments later, when the effects of the beam had worn off, Dewilde ran towards the craft but it took off before he reached it.

French scientists who investigated the sighting estimated an object of about 35 tonnes had rested on the railway track.

Both Valensole and Quarouble are typical of those who claim to have seen alien beings at first hand. The same description of the creatures has been repeated time and time again by people scattered all over the globe.

Take the experience of Danie Van Graan who, while walking near Loxton, South Africa, in July 1975, came upon what he at first thought was an aluminium caravan. As he drew closer, Van Graan saw that

CLOSEST ENCOUNTERS

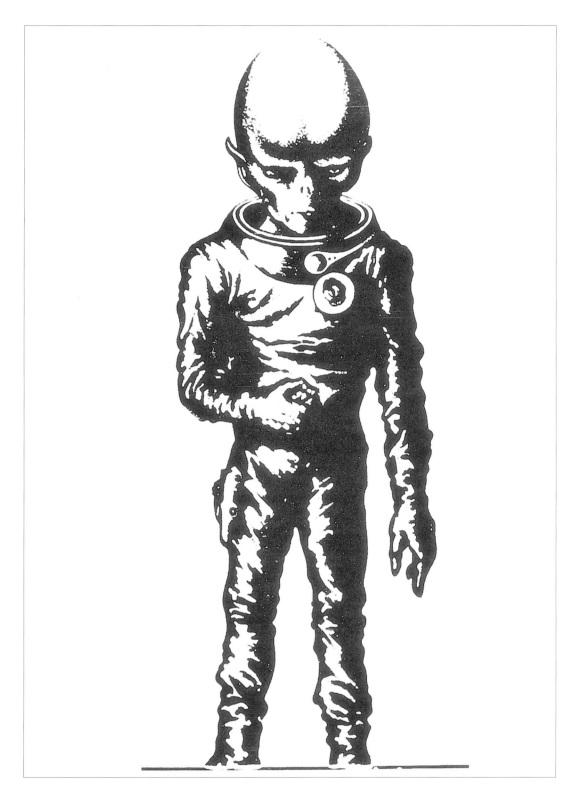

Typical UFO occupant, based on work by scientists using 300 landing cases

it was made of a curious silvery, metallic substance and inside figures could be seen moving about. They were small and thin, with high cheekbones and slanted eyes. They wore simple, one-piece suits of a cream colour.

He approached the object from an earth bank which was about 3 metres/10 feet high. When he got to within 6 metres/20 feet of it, a beam of light flashed from the craft and dazed him. At the same time, his nose began to bleed. Through his blurred vision — it was impaired for years after the event — he saw the craft take off from the alfalfa field about 20 seconds later. As in the Valensole case, crops would not grow in the immediate landing area for some time afterwards.

In the same year, across the Indian Ocean on Reunion Island, an almost identical experience was met by a man named Antoine Severin. He came upon a domed UFO in a field and observed several beings about 122 cm/4 feet tall. They fired at him with a beam weapon and knocked him unconscious.

When he came to, both his sight and speech were impaired. The condition lasted several days and was attributed to shock by a psychiatrist who examined him. A Lieutenant Colonel Lobet of the local police later wrote in his report that Severin was 'normally a well-balanced, well-behaved individual of excellent character and not given to the perpetration of hoaxes'.

None of the subjects in these encounters was seriously hurt or suffered lasting damage as a result of the light-ray. The accounts are simple and, it would seem, unelaborate compared to some of the more exotic stories of alien abduction and genetic experiments.

As a footnote, an object similar to the one seen by Maurice Masse was spotted by another French farmer, Renato Nicolai, in 1981 in the village of Trans-en-Provence. Nikolai had been working outside at around 5 pm when he heard a whistling sound above him and saw an egg-shaped craft the size of a small car descending nearby. It touched down on a nearby slope and he began to walk towards it.

After a few moments it took off again, hovered at around 6 metres/20 feet and sped off to the north-east, as if it had been disturbed by the farmer's presence.

SECRETS OF
RENDLESHAM FOREST

A squad of terrified servicemen, a herd of cows which went berserk and strange lights in the sky. These are some of the ingredients in what may have been the most significant UFO event since Roswell. Just as in 1947, it occurred in an area ringed by secret military installations and nuclear facilities. This time it was to be on British soil.

The affair began on Boxing Night 1980 in a small plantation of pine trees called Rendlesham Forest, eight miles north of Ipswich. To the north are the controversial Sizewell nuclear power plants; to the south is a military communications centre at Martlesham Heath, and RAF Bawdsey, where secret radar research is carried out.

On the coast, Orford Ness is home to secret US research units linked to the National Security Agency. In the heart of the forest are two air bases, RAF Woodbridge and Bentwaters. In 1980 these were still being leased by the US and staffed by hundreds of USAF personnel.

Between 9 pm and 3 am the next morning there were several seemingly inexplicable events. To begin with, passenger flights flying over the area reported large numbers of comets or shooting stars. At Sudbourne, a man saw a huge flowing ball pass overhead to vanish into the forest. And on a back road between Orford and Woodbridge, a courting couple saw a flash of light as something plunged out of the sky into the trees.

What they could not have known was that the object they had seen was being tracked by radar at RAF Watton, 50 miles away, and at Bentwaters base. Moments after the 'crash', Woodbridge base went on full alert. It was 3 am on the morning of 27 December.

Locals say there was pandemonium as jeeps and lorries roared out of the base in search of the UFO. Speculation abounded later, and elements of the story were leaked to at least two groups of UFOlogists by USAF servicemen. But there was silence from both the British Ministry of Defence and the Americans.

Then in 1983 a memo written by one a senior base officer a few days after the event was released under the US Freedom of Information Act. It created an immediate sensation, describing how air force security men had seen unusual lights outside the back gate of the base and went to investigate. It stated:

'They reported seeing a strange glowing object in the forest. The object was described as metallic in appearance and triangular in shape, approximately two to three meters (6 ½ feet to nearly 10 feet) across the base and approximately two meters high. It illuminated the entire forest with a white light. The object itself had a pulsing red light on top and a bank of blue lights underneath. The object was hovering or on legs. As the patrolmen approached the object, it manoeuvred through the trees and disappeared. At this time, the animals on a nearby farm went into a frenzy. The object was briefly sighted about an hour later near the back gate'.

But that was not the end. Later in the night, according to the memo, a red sun-like object was seen through the trees. It broke into five pieces and disappeared. Immediately afterwards, three star-like objects were seen low in the sky, two to the north and one to the south. They displayed red, green and blue lights. The one in the north was visible for an hour or more, the two in the south for a period of two to three hours.

Next day, the forest site was thoroughly investigated. Small dents in the ground were found, suggesting the object was on legs, and radiation levels in the surrounding area were higher than normal. There was damage to the trees immediately above, as if a large object had crashed through the forest canopy.

Even more startling claims about that night's events have come from one of the patrol members, source of the leak to UFOlogists. He said: 'It was lit up like a Christmas tree with white lights and a blue bank

FACT OR FICTION?: UFOs

Examining alleged UFO landing site (top)   UFOs photographed over Conisbrough, South Yorkshire (bottom)

of lights. It moved slowly at first, but then it moved so fast and it turned at right angles in an impossible way. I do not know any technology that could do the things this did. It was just like magic'.

He claimed to have seen small creatures — possibly robots — with domed heads suspended in a beam of light beneath the object repairing the craft. Base commander Gordon Williams was called out to attempt to communicate with the creatures using sign language. The patrolman said it seemed almost as if the craft had been expected. The UFO had been damaged as it fell through the trees but was quickly repaired and the aliens left.

All sorts of theories have since been advanced to explain the sighting. Sceptics suggest the UFO was a meteor and the white light nothing more than the lighthouse on Orford Ness shining through the trees. More fanciful explanations suggest the testing of top-secret psychic mind-rays or of high-tech satellite propulsion systems. Others speculate that the UFO story was a cover for more sinister events, perhaps a nuclear leak.

Confronted with the officer's memorandum, the British Ministry of Defence admitted that Lieutenant Colonel Holt's story was true and that there was no rational explanation for what had happened. Ralph Noyes, former head of the Whitehall department responsible for investigating UFOs, has summed up the dilemma facing the MoD in dealing with the Rendlesham affair:

'It embarrasses them. Either they must admit that a senior USAF officer at a highly sensitive base in the United Kingdom went out of his mind in December 1980 (with unthinkable potential consequences in defence terms) or they must acknowledge publicly that weird things occur for which no explanation is at present possible'.

Still more puzzling is a tape recording allegedly made by Lieutenant Colonel Holt that night, which apparently describes the search through the woods as it happened and a moment of terror as the alien craft began firing beams of white light at the patrol. It was released by a former base commander at RAF Woodbridge in 1984. Most UFOlogists suspect that the so-called Holt Tape is probably not genuine.

No film or photographs of what happened have ever been released, although it is said the entire episode was filmed by an officer with a video camera. Stories of car engines mysteriously cutting out and of strange lights in the area continue to be reported.

The final and perhaps most puzzling word on the affair is a comment made by Lord Trefgarne on behalf of Michael Heseltine, who was then Defence Secretary. Asked about the Rendlesham Incident by Lord Hill-Norton, the former Chief of Defence Staff, Lord Trefgarne's rather cryptic reply was: 'The events to which you refer were of no defence significance'.

GIANTS IN THE PARK

One of the strangest and — if true — most significant encounters of modern times took place in a park in the Russian city of Voronezh in September 1989. It was late afternoon and dusk was closing in when a group of children playing football saw a ball of fire circle the area and settle on a tree. From within emerged an alien more than 3 metres/10 feet tall.

A Tass news agency report of the incident was flashed around the world — it was not an organisation noted for its sense of humour — and made headlines everywhere.

The story was taken most seriously by Soviet authorities. Their military flights and their top-secret installations had for years been buzzed by UFOs, just as those of the Americans had been. For many years, the official communist view had been that Unidentified Flying Objects were a capitalist con trick designed to destabilise Soviet society. But after hundreds of sightings, official resolve began to weaken.

Five years before the Voronezh encounter, the Kremlin ordered the formation of a special investigation team to probe the UFO phenomenon. The move was sparked by a string of sightings over restricted airspace. Indeed, there is some suggestion that the Korean Airlines jumbo jet shot down over Sakhalin Island in 1983 might have been mistaken for one.

The Soviets had even had their own equivalent of the Roswell incident. In 1986 a 'flying sphere' was seen to crash into a mountain called Hill 611, near the village of Dalnegorsk in the Vladivostok area.

The object disintegrated upon impact but investigators from the Academy of Sciences did find some debris, including a strange mesh material and a previously unknown chromium alloy. Was it a rogue space probe, as some suggested, or something more sinister?

Three years later came UFO sightings over Voronezh which culminated in the landing, or possibly landings, in the park.

Reports of the aliens generally describe them as being unusually tall (most American and European sightings involve beings of between 120 cm and 150 cm/4 and 5 feet high. In comparison to the rest of their bodies, their heads were tiny and they had three eyes. Their skin, according to one child, was 'the colour of grilled beefburger' and they wore silver suits. One alien walked around the park, accompanied by a small robot-like machine, before returning to his craft and taking off again. A second craft carrying another two aliens touched down shortly afterwards.

What is less widely known is that the landing was one of several alleged to have taken place over the period. Dr Henry Silanov, of Voronezh Geological-Geophysical laboratory later reported:

'In the period between 21 September and 28 October 1989, in Western Park in Voronezh, six landings and one sighting (hovering) were registered, with the appearances of walking beings. We have collected a wealth of video materials with eyewitness accounts, particularly from pupils of the nearest school. We have no doubts that they are telling the truth in their accounts'.

One child witness, Vasya Surin, was in the park on the evening of 29 September. He saw a pink haze hover over a nearby building and stopped to watch it with his friends. From the middle of the haze came a red, glowing sphere which buzzed around the park, eventually hovering over a poplar tree. Surin's tale continues: 'A door opened in the sphere while it hovered. A person looked out. He was tall, about 3 metres (approximately 9 feet 8 inches), shone silvery, and his arms were down to his knees. His head was just a continuation of his shoulders, with three eyes: two at the sides and a third just a little higher up'.

The craft settled on the tree and the alien climbed down and walked around. He flashed a pistol-like device at a man walking towards a bus-stop, which made the man disappear, says Surin. Moments after the craft left, the man reappeared, with no recollection of the occurence (there is no evidence available from the man in question). After the first alien took off again, the second UFO descended containing two more beings. They too got out of their craft and investigated a line of electricity pylons.

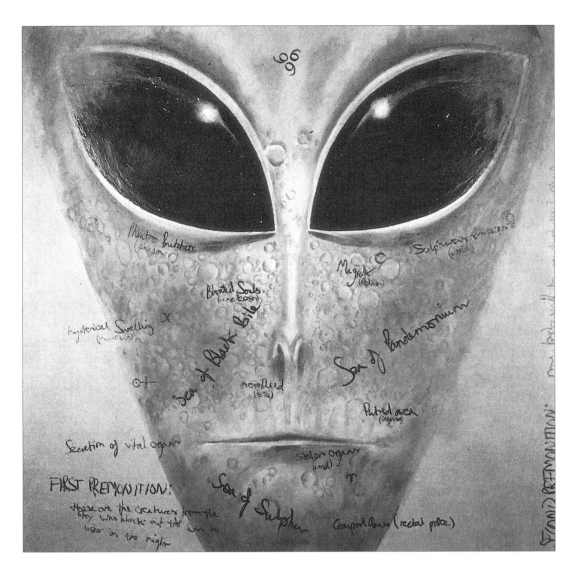

'Grey' alien entity, as portrayed by Rod Dickinson

That something happened that afternoon is undeniable. But the biggest weakness is that so much of the eyewitness evidence is from schoolchildren aged between 13 and 16. Did they embellish upon a straightforward UFO sighting?

Significantly, a local militiaman Lieutenant Sergei Matveyev, describes how he saw an object over the park that evening and rubbed his eyes in disbelief. It was about 165 metres/50 feet wide. But, he insists, he did not see it land – nor did he see aliens.

Another adult witness to events at Voronezh was Denis Murzenko, who had gone for an early evening stroll a few days earlier. He saw a pink egg-shaped object descending from the sky. It was swaying like a leaf from side to side as it did so (this description is a classic account of a UFO landing). Inside the machine, it was possible to see a humanoid: 'The person seemed to be about four and a half feet (about 140 cm) high', he said later. 'I stood still and it kept coming down lower and lower. I became frightened and ran off'.

Just as is the case in other encounters, the passing of time makes a true analysis of events in Voronezh extremely difficult. To begin with, the children's description of even the location of the landing is vaguein the extreme.

Certain evidence has a hollow ring to it. Some observers claim to have seen the symbol for the planet Uranus on the underside of the craft, the so-called Ummo symbol. This seems extremely unlikely.

Other contradictions emerged when the area was checked for radiation. Dr Silvanov was quoted by the news agency Tass as saying that two pieces of a sandstone-type rock had been found in the park and that 'mineralogical analysis has shown that the substance cannot be found on Earth'.

The following day, the good doctor was refuting his initial claim; the rock was a simple iron ore.

It was not long before tours of the UFO landing site were being organised for 60 roubles a head. Perhaps it is not surprising that Soviet and European television crews who showed up to investigate the events were unable to find adult witnesses willing to talk. The whole thing was rapidly turning to farce.

If the Rendlesham and Roswell incidents are anything to go by, it may be many years before the whole truth of what happened in Voronezh Park is revealed.

SHOCKING ENCOUNTERS

THE BETTY CASH SAGA

Restaurant boss Betty Cash might have saved herself years of pain had she decided to stay in the night of 29 December 1980. Instead she drove out on business with a member of her staff, Vickie Landrum, to inspect a rival restaurant which had just opened. Landrum brought her seven-year-old grandson Colby with her. They were driving through pine woods near Dayton, Texas when they spotted a huge diamond-shaped object just above tree-top height and about 30 metres/100 feet away. It was about 9 pm. Cash slammed on the brakes and got out of the car with her work colleague to take a look.

They immediately felt a burning sensation on their faces and noticed what appeared to be flames coming from beneath the object. Both describe a roaring noise, like a flame-thrower, and a series of bleeps accompanying it.

Colby was screaming hysterically for the two women to get back in the car, which they did after a few moments. Landrum recalls that when her hand touched the dashboard it left an imprint. When Cash tried to get back in the car, she found she could scarcely grasp the door handle because it was so hot.

They started the engine and began to follow the UFO, which was now rising slowly into the sky. As it did so, they counted 23 helicopters which appeared out of the darkness and seemed to surround it. Cash estimated the stand-off distance at about 2 km/¾ mile.

The object began to move off, with the helicopters — later identified as twin-rotored Chinook C-47s — maintaining their distance. Eventually, they werelost to sight. Within hours the three people in the car were all suffering bizarre, painful symptoms.

Colby had a burned face and serious eye inflammation. Landrum was similarly affected, and she also suffered temporary hair loss. There were odd indentations on her fingernails also. However, it was Cash who suffered most. Her symptoms included blinding headaches and neck pains, diarrhoea, nausea and vomiting, and eye inflammation. There were blisters on her scalp, too.

Unable to walk and almost unconscious, she was taken to hospital in Houston four days later, where she was treated as a burns victim. There was little improvement, however. She was sent home but was back in hospital almost immediately.

Her hair began falling out in clumps. She developed breast cancer and had to undergo a mastectomy operation. The two women eventually decided to sue the government for what was then the equivalent of £20 million, on the grounds that the flying object must have been US property and it was responsible for their injuries.

The case went on for several years in Houston District Court. Representatives of NASA, the air force, army and navy were all called to give evidence. The suit was dismissed in 1986.

The judge's verdict was that no such flying object was owned or operated by the government — and the Chinooks' ownership remains a mystery. In 1991 Cash's doctor told newsmen that her symptoms were a textbook case of radiation sickness. It was as if she had been exposed to an unshielded nuclear reactor or had been standing 5 to 8 km/3 to 5 miles from the epicentre of the Hiroshima A-bomb.

Rumours persist in the region that the helicopters had been escorting an experimental craft of some sort. Could it be that the Cash-Landrum encounter was with an experimental RPV, or remotely piloted vehicle, powered by a nuclear reactor or carrying nuclear weapons? Robotised military machines have been talked about for many years.

In 1983 a US Army report confidently predicted: 'Remote-controlled flying saucers and robot-guided vehicles will be used on battlefields'.

Evidence to support the theory comes from Britain, where there have been several reports of diamond-shaped or triangular-shaped UFOs. One such sighting occurred in the Barnsley area of Yorkshire on the morning of 20 April 1988.

Two witnesses walking across farmland north-east of the town saw a large triangular-shaped object in the sky. Nearby was a man in a car who appeared to be manoeuvring the object using a control box.

A fleet of four or five cars sped off in pursuit of the object at the same time as the man with the control drove off. But what did Betty Cash see? The F-117a Stealth fighter, which first entered service in 1977 but whose existence was not admitted by the USAF until 1988, has a bizarre, triangular appearance — just as Betty Cash had reported.

Work on the Stealth project had been going on since 1966 and numerous prototypes were made — one early Lockheed design, for example, was known as the XST and was capable of Mach 2. Even after this fighter entered service, work was still continuing on the B-2 Stealth bomber which did not enter service until the late Eighties.

Could Betty Cash have seen an early prototype of a Stealth aircraft, perhaps one with vertical takeoff and landing capabilities? She would perhaps not be the first person to have come across a machine which she was not supposed to see.

In 1964, a cop chasing a speeding car had a close encounter with a UFO which had apparently landed in the scrublands of New Mexico, near Socorro. Patrolman Lonnie Zamora gave up chasing the speeder after hearing a loud explosion.

He turned off to investigate, thinking a nearby dynamite store had exploded. What he found was a shiny oval object parked about 183 metres/200 yards off the main road.

Outside it were two people in white overalls, who seemed startled to see him. They got inside their vehicle and took off in a column of flame. Zamora watched the machine level off and fly horizontally into the distance.

Later investigations revealed scorched earth where the vehicle had been. The cop's testimony remained unshakeable and was supported by witnesses who had seen him veer off the road towards the UFO.

Many UFOlogists now believe that what the officer saw was in fact some sort of experimental spacecraft, perhaps a prototype of the lunar module.

The big difference is that Patrolman Zamora suffered no ill effects afterwards. Betty Cash's ordeal, on the other hand, turned her life into a living nightmare.

THE VANISHING AUSTRALIAN

Since the start of the last century, there have been numerous cases of groups and individuals who have disappeared in the wake of UFO encounters. The story of the first 4th Norfolk Regiment, for instance, has gone down in legend. Nearly 1000 men marched into a strange cloud over Hill 60 at Gallipoli, Turkey, in August 1915, never to be seen again. Such unexplained disappearances are very rare but do happen.

Such was the case of amateur pilot Frederick Valentich. The last time he was seen, he was preparing to take off from Morrabin Airport, Melbourne. What happened that day in October 1978 remains a mystery but he never returned from his flight across the Bass Strait to King Island. And no wreckage of his blue and white Cessna 182 has yet been recovered. What has survived is the transcript of his radio conversations with air traffic controllers that evening.

The drama began at 7.06pm, almost an hour after take-off, when Valentich radioed the controllers to report a large aircraft flying within sight of him at around 1525 metres/5000 feet. His call sign was *Delta Sierra Juliet*. The following are extracts from the radio exchanges, which were punctuated by curious metallic noises. *See panel opposite*

7:06
Control: What type of aircraft is it?
DSJ: I cannot affirm. It is four bright . . . it seems to me like landing lights.

7:07
DSJ: Melbourne, this is *Delta Sierra Juliet*. The aircraft has just passed over me, at least a thousand feet above.
Control: *Delta Sierra Juliet*, roger. And it is a large aircraft, confirmed?
DSJ: Er . . . unknown, due to the speed it's travelling. Is there any air force activity in the vicinity?
Control: *Delta Sierra Juliet*, no known aircraft in the vicinity.

7:08
DSJ: Melbourne, it's approaching now from due east towards me . . . it seems to me that he's playing some sort of game. He's flying over me – two, three times – at speeds I could not identify.

7:09
DSJ: Melbourne, *Delta Sierra Juliet*. It's not an aircraft. It is . . .
Control: *Delta Sierra Juliet*, can you describe the — er — aircraft?
DSJ: *Delta Sierra Juliet*, as it's flying past it's a long shape. . . cannot identify it more than it has such speed. . . It's before me right now, Melbourne.

7:10
Control: *Delta Sierra Juliet*: and how large would the — er — object be?
DSJ: *Delta Sierra Juliet*, Melbourne. It seems like it's stationary. What I'm doing right now is . . . orbiting and the thing is just orbiting on top of me also. It's got a green light and sort of metallic-like. It's all shiny on the outside...
Control: *Delta Sierra Julie*t.
DSJ: *Delta Sierra Juliet* (five second pause). It's just vanished.
Control: *Delta Sierra Juliet*.

7:11
DSJ: Melbourne, would you know what kind of aircraft I've got. Is it a military aircraft?
Control: *Delta Sierra Juliet*, confirm the — er — aircraft just vanished.
DSJ: Say again.
Control: *Delta Sierra Juliet*, is the aircraft still with you?
DSJ: Delta Sierra Juliet, it's now approaching from the south-west.
Control: *Delta Sierra Juliet*.
DSJ: *Delta Sierra Juliet*. The engine is rough-idling. I've got it set at twenty-three/twenty-four and the thing is coughing.
Control: *Delta Sierra Juliet*, roger. What are your intentions?
DSJ: My intentions are — ah — to go to King Island — ah — Melbourne. That strange aircraft is hovering on top of me again (two second pause). It is hovering and it's not an aircraft.
Control: *Delta Sierra Juliet*.
DSJ: *Delta Sierra Juliet*, Melbourne (microphone left open for 17 seconds — radio contact lost.)

Disappearance of Fredrick Valentich, Bass Strait of Victoria, Australia, October 1978 (top)
Martians' footprints in the sand (bottom)

The Bass Strait triangle has long been a source of UFO sightings, on the Australian mainland and in Tasmania, across the water.

In February 1975, two campers on a fishing trip to Tasmania's Lake Sorrell saw a UFO dive from the night sky and hover over the water. Its brilliant lights continued to illuminate the area for several moments after it disappeared. There have been other reports of sightings which stopped car and truck engines in their tracks.

The Valentich case coincided with a glut of sightings. For several days the local UFO group had been inundated with calls. But the most interesting testimony came from a bank manager and his wife who had been driving near Melbourne on the evening of the disappearance. They had seen a green, starfish-shaped object flying out to sea in the same area as the ill-fated Cessna went missing.

There have been numerous local rumours about what happened to Valentich and his plane. One group of divers claimed to have found the wreck at the bottom of the Straits and taken pictures of it. That turned out to be a hoax. Another story had Valentich alive and well and working in a petrol station in Tasmania.

There has been much speculation about the fact that Valentich had a keen interest in UFOs. Indeed he carried a scrapbook of cuttings with him on the flight. Some say that he may even have arranged his own disappearance using the UFO story as his cover.

The official air accident investigation report merely arrived at these two rather obvious conclusions:

1   Degree of injury — presumed fatal

2   Opinion as to cause — the reason for the disappearance of the aircraft has not been determined

Eight years after the Valentich case, a Japanese Airlines 747 cargo plane had an extraordinarily similar encounter, this time over Alaska. The date, 17 November 1986. Pilot Kenju Terauchi spotted lights in the distance and, just as Valentich had done, thought they were a military aircraft. As they closed on it, the pilot and his two officers saw two craft, each about the same size as a DC-8 jet.

They were moving about 300 metres/1000 feet in front of the jumbo jet. Terauchi contacted Anchorage flight control, which called up a nearby Air Force radar station to check its scopes. The objects were tracked by both the Air Force and the 747's own on-board radar. After about half an hour, the first two UFOs disappeared into the distance and another pale white light began to shine behind the 747. It was emanating from a craft which Terauchi estimated to be the size of two aircraft carriers — perhaps some sort of mother ship. It vanished moments later, leaving the crew to land their plane, which by now was dangerously low on fuel.

They were lucky. Valentich, it would seem, was not.

THE WELSH TRIANGLE

Tales of Unidentified Flying Objects can bring out the worst in people. Such stories are, after all, excellent newspaper and television material. And the thought of celebrity status is enough to turn many perfectly normal people into consummate hoaxers.

If any proof of this is needed, it is to be found in a remarkable chain of events which took place in a quiet, rural corner of Dyfed, Wales in the spring and summer of 1977. The area was to become known as the Welsh Triangle and the incidents which occurred were, to all and sundry, the Pembrokeshire Flap. It is a shocking story, to be sure but, as most UFOlogists agree, the shocking behaviour was entirely human.

This part of Britain is, of course, no stranger to the paranormal, with a mythical past which takes in characters such as Merlin and turn of the century preacher Mary Jones, who could allegedly summon up lights in the sky.

The Flap began with a group of children at Broad Haven primary school rushing to tell their teachers that they had seen a UFO in a nearby field. When the teachers refused to investigate, the children signed a petition stating what they had seen and went to the local police station. It should be noted at this point that the children's sighting followed others on previous days at two schools in the neighbouring villages of Penarth and Hubberston.

Subsequent investigation of the area where the Broad Haven craft was said to have landed showed it was covered in scrub and bushes, and that any sighting there could only have been partial.

This did not concern The Western Telegraph unduly. It knew a good story when it saw one and sent staff down to interview the pupils. As locals began to realise that the event was being taken seriously, they began to reveal other tales of strange lights in the sky and mysterious craft landing in fields.

As one local investigator, Randall Jones Pugh, said at the time: 'People are beginning to come forward now that they realise nobody is going to take the mickey out of them'.

The newspapers even established a name for the area — The Welsh Triangle — which sounded very dramatic in headlines. The tone of the accounts was rarely critical. Almost anyone who came forward with a story was given a hearing. As the national newspapers got involved, the tone was increasingly one of hysteria.

Thirteen-year-old Debra Swan was determined to find one of the space vehicles. So on the evening of 14 April she set off across the local park with her friends. Two of them became frightened and ran home. The others went on, across a potato field and down a bank. There was something in the field in front of them. Deborah said later:

'I have never seen anything like it before in my life. I thought it was my eyes playing a trick at first, but it wasn't. The most astonishing thing about it was the colour, which was a brilliant gleaming silver. The shape was like a football . . . it moved at all angles: backwards, forwards, left to right. As we moved, it moved as well. We then ran back as fast as we could'.

Incredibly this story of a little girl searching for a UFO and actually finding one was taken at face value by journalists.

The tales continued to spew forth. Many of them were linked to the Coombs family, who lived at Ripperston Farm. Their cottage was next door to that of a couple called Brian and Caroline Klass, who were never questioned about any of the bizarre events their neighbours claimed had happened.

Cows which were teleported during the night, cars which were destroyed by an inexplicable electromagnetic force and television sets which blew up. These are just some of the stories which appeared in the newspapers but which were the subject of much local hilarity.

The cars Mr Coombs was said to have bought were bangers anyway, they said. Not surprising they conked out. The cows wandered because the gates were left open. The electricity bills were astronomical because they left their doors and windows open.

There is no doubt that something strange did happen on the night of 23 April. Mr Coombs rang his farm manager in the middle of the night, clearly frightened. His wife had seen a sinister 'entity' at the window. But, says local gossip, it was merely a couple of practical jokers who had already pulled such a stunt on the owner of the Haven Fort Hotel, who had claimed a UFO sighting herself.

Later that year, Pauline Coombs claimed to have seen another UFO flying over Stack Rocks, an outcrop a couple of miles offshore. She also claimed to have seen figures moving about on the rocks. Subsequent investigation suggests that she was probably too far to be able to see such detail clearly. Her credibility as a witness was further diminished when she later claimed to have been taken aboard a spaceship.

So what are we to make of the Welsh Triangle? There were dozens of alleged sightings, virtually all of which have been revealed to be flawed in some fundamental way. This is the consensus of UFOlogists who have studied the events of that year.

A handful of incidents, however, remain intriguing. Such a case is that of Josephine Hewison, who was standing at her bedroom window one March morning at Lower Broadmoor Farm. She looked out across a field in front of the house and saw an object measuring about 15 metres/50 feet across. It was disc-shaped and – in Mrs Hewison's own words – looked rather like a 'squashed jelly mould'. She stood there transfixed for more than two minutes, then ran to tell her children. When she returned she saw that the object had gone.

She insists the incident did not frighten her in any way, unlike newspaper reports which described her as 'terrified'.

There are some rather interesting parallels between the Welsh Triangle and the supposed alien landings at Voronezh in the Soviet Union some ten years later. In both cases, children were the instigators of the first reports. Subsequently, press and television raised the local level of awareness and more and more people came forward with taller and taller stories about what they have seen.

It is a guaranteed recipe for confusion and deceit.

MAN-MADE SAUCERS

There have been many attempts to explain the existence of UFOs. Most of these have suggested extra-terrestrial origins. There is, however, a degree of evidence to support the claim that they are man-made devices.

One leading exponent of the theory is UFO writer W A Harbinson, whose recent book *Projekt UFO* analyses the history of aerodynamics and particularly the experiments carried out in Hitler's Germany upon 'flying wing' and saucer-shaped aircraft. This technology was later expropriated by the United States and the Soviet Union and was further developed in the late 1940s and 1950s.

The 'flying wing' developed as an attempt to confront the problem of the so-called boundary layer of air which envelopes any flying body. As aircraft flew closer to the sound barrier, drag from the boundary layer became a major hindrance.

Aero-engineers of the period knew that one way of solving the problem would be to create a wing surface which combined aerofoil and propulsion systems in a single unit. In practice this meant a v-shaped wing or a disc-shaped craft whose jet turbines were mounted along its circumference. There is some suggestion that the Foo Fighters seen by allied pilots during World War Two may have been radio-controlled flying discs of this type.

Harbinson speculates further that the US and possibly Canadian governments constructed manned craft for policing their sub-polar regions, which would have been prime targets in the event of war with Russia. Indeed, the Canadian firm AVRO did make public a prototype 'flying saucer' in the 1960s, although it never got more than a few feet off the ground.

A fully developed flying disc would – in theory at least – be capable of enormous acceleration and very high speeds.

Harbinson's theory would go some way to explaining why so many UFOs are seen over secret military bases. It would also explain why the US government has at various times remained remarkably unperturbed by what seemed to be sinister and serious UFO encounters over sensitive sites — Washington in 1952 is a prime example.

Nevertheless it seems unlikely any government would be able to keep such technology a secret from the rest of the world for 50 years or more.

SINISTER ENCOUNTERS

THE CLOSEST
ENCOUNTER OF ALL

The story of Antonio Villas Boas is the stuff of fantasy. A tale of abduction, a strange spacecraft and a sexual encounter with a beautiful alien being. Yet this poor Brazilian farmer managed to convince both doctors and psychologists that he was telling the truth.

The impact of his tale, coupled with other sightings over Brazil forced even the country's secret service to sit up and taken notice. The whole extraordinary episode began in Rio de Janeiro on the afternoon of 22 February 1958 when Villas Boas presented himself at the surgery of Dr Olavo Fontes.

He made a detailed and lengthy statement which was witnessed by the doctor and by a journalist, Joao Martins, who was developing an interest in Brazilian UFOs. He had helped Villas Boas, who was anxious to explain his experiences to civil and military authorities, to come to Rio.

Villas Boas's family farm was near Sao Francisco de Sales in the state of Minas Gerais. He was single, in good health and shared the business with his two brothers. He had witnessed strange lights over the farm on various occasions starting on the night of 5 October 1957. A week later while working in a field with one of his brothers he saw a brilliant white light on the ground.

When he approached, it turned red and sped to the other end of the field, then disappeared as if it had been switched off. But it was the events of the following night which were to achieve a unique place in the annals of UFOlogy. Villas Boas was working with a tractor alone in the field when a brilliant light raced across the sky and hovered 45 metres/150 feet above him.

After two minutes, it landed in front of him and he could see it was a large egg-shaped object with red lights all around it. It stood upon three landing legs each about 9 metres/30 feet high. Up until now, the farmer had been rooted to the spot, not knowing what to do next. Suddenly, he put his foot down on the tractor accelerator in an attempt to flee. He managed to travel only a few feet before the motor and headlights went dead.

Boas jumped down and attempted to run away but was grabbed by the arm. He looked down to see a small, strangely-dressed being holding onto him. He pushed the creature to the ground but three others appeared and managed to restrain him. They dragged him up a boarding ladder into the craft and took him into a brilliantly-lit room.

There were five creatures in total and they appeared to be conversing in a strange language about Villas Boas. Each wore close-fitting overalls of a thick, grey material. They wore five-fingered gloves. They also wore helmets through which Boas could make out their blue eyes.

They began removing his clothes and rubbed him down with a clear, odourless fluid. They led him naked to another room where another two of the aliens appeared to take a blood sample from him. The ends of two tubes were attached by suction to his chin.

Villas Boas described the procedure as painless but the skin was sore afterwards. He watched a small beaker fill with his own blood, then the aliens, seemingly satisfied, walked out and left him alone. He had sat alone and terrified for about half an hour when the door opened and a woman came slowly towards him.

She was blonde (Villas Boas said her hair had a bleached appearance) and strikingly beautiful, with large blue eyes and high cheekbones. Her chin was so pointed that her face had a triangular aspect. Her pubic hair was a brilliant red.

The rather bashful farmer described what happened next.

'She had the most beautiful body which I have ever seen on a woman, with high, well-shaped breasts and narrow waist. She was broad in the hips, had long thighs and small feet, narrow hands and normal finger-nails. She was much smaller than I am, and her head only reached to my shoulder. Alone with this woman, who clearly gave me to understand what it was that she wanted, I became very excited . . . I forgot everything, seized the woman and responded to her caresses. It was a normal act and she behaved like any other woman.

'I would not like to exchange her for one of our women, for I prefer a woman with whom one can talk and who understands one. I was also irritated by the grunting sounds she made at particular moments. She did not know how to kiss either, unless her playful bites on my chin had the same meaning'.

Before leaving him, the alien pointed to her belly and to the stars — suggesting to the farmer that she would bear his child in space. Shortly afterward, another of the beings returned with his clothes and he put them back on.

He was taken on a guided tour of the craft by one of the crew. He was shown the central dome, which emitted a strange green light and which he was given to understand played a key part in the propulsion system. After another while, he was taken to the ladder and one of the beings indicated he was free to go.

A short while later, the craft took off towards the south. It was 5.30 am. Villas Boas had gone aboard at approximately 1.15 am.

For days after the encounter, the farmer suffered from nausea, headaches and an unpleasant burning sensation in his eyes. He was too excited even to sleep yet. He told no-one apart from his mother what had happened – she told him to have nothing more to do with such people. Later, after reading an article about UFOs in a publication called Cruzeiro, he approached the journalist Joao Martins, who paid part of his fare to Rio.

In his subsequent medical and psychological evaluation of Villas Boas, Dr Fontes found no signs whatsoever that the man was suffering from mental disorder. Indeed, he was impressed with the lucidity of his descriptions.

He also found damaged areas of skin around the chin, at the points where the farmer said blood had been taken, and there was evidence of irritation around his fingernails and along his arms. Both Dr Fontes and other doctors who examined Villas Boas agreed that this irritation, along with the other symptoms that the man experienced, were classic indications of radiation sickness. That was a fact not even the most extravagant imagination could manufacture.

Boas was not a drug addict. He was in perfect health at the time of the encounter and was studying at evening classes to improve the lot of himself and his family. His work evidently paid off because by 1978, he had become the respected Dr Villas Boas, a lawyer living near Brasilia with his wife and four children. He broke his silence that year in an interview with Brazilian television in which he explained that after sex, the alien had collected a sperm sample from him. He died in 1990, claiming that the United States had 30 years earlier invited him to examine the wreckage of one of their UFOs.

Since Villas Boas, there have been hundreds of claimed abductions. However, many depend on the flimsiest of evidence, such as so-called regression analysis in which hypnotic techniques are used to take the subject's unconscious mind back to the time when the events happened. At least 50 per cent of the abduction cases reported to UFOlogists depend entirely upon evidence produced from regression.

The following cases are typical:

> • 4 May 1969, Belo Horizonte, Brazil   Soldier Jose Antonio da Silva is fishing in the afternoon when he becomes aware of figures moving behind him. He is seized by two aliens, both about 120 cm/4 feet tall wearing silver suits and metal helmets. He is taken in their craft to another location where the bodies of four human beings are presented to him. A message is given to him in Portuguese which he still refuses to divulge. Four days later, the craft takes off again and deposits him in Victoria, nearly 325 km/200 miles from where he started. Cynics suggest he dreamed up the abduction to explain his four-day absence.

• 5 November 1975, Snowflake, Arizona   A woodcutting team working in a national park sees a UFO hovering over the trees. One of them, Travis Walton, jumps from his truck and races towards it. His friends flee the area after they see Walton is struck by a ray from the craft. When police arrive, Walton is nowhere to be found. He eventually shows up five days later claiming he had been taken aboard the spacecraft. The story becomes the subject of a major feature film. Critics point to Walton's previous criminal record and suggest the story may have been fabricated to save the woodcutters from incurring a contract penalty.

• 3 October 1978, Sayama City, Japan   CB radio enthusiast Hideicho Amano drives with his two-year-old daughter to the top of a mountain to get better reception on his car set. He was suddenly aware of the car being bathed in light and realises that his daughter is lying across the back seat with an orange beam directed at her stomach. He attempts to retrieve her but is prevented by a hideous, noseless being who renders him temporarily paralysed. The creature departs and Amano flees the area. Later he is aware of strange images and voices in his mind and believes the aliens will return.

• 3 January 1979, Mindalore, Johannesburg   Mother Meagan Quezet and her son walk out late at night to retrieve their dog. They stumble upon a craft on landing legs emitting a strange pink glow. Five or six bearded figures appear, speaking a Chinese-like language before taking off. Regression analysis later suggests that both mother and son were taken aboard the craft.

• 28 November 1980, Todmorden, West Yorkshire   Policeman Godfrey Todmorden is driving through the countryside in the early hours to investigate reports of stray cattle. He sees what at first appears to be a bus ahead of him. It is in fact a large dome-shaped object hovering over the road. Todmorden's car and personal radios fail when he attempts to call for help. Regression analysis suggests he was taken aboard the craft and subjected to some form of medical examination.

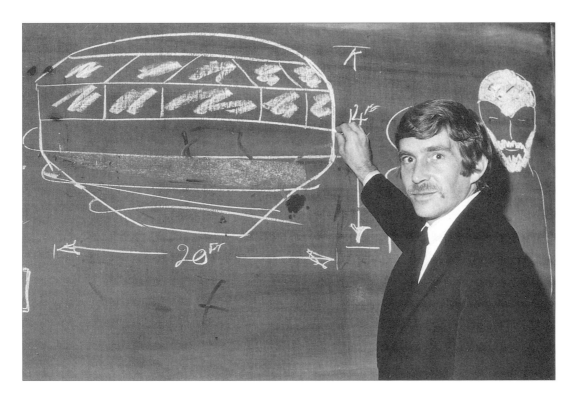

PC Alan Godfrey, UFO abductee, Manchester 1982 (top)   Writing seen by Villas Boas above door of spacecraft (bottom)

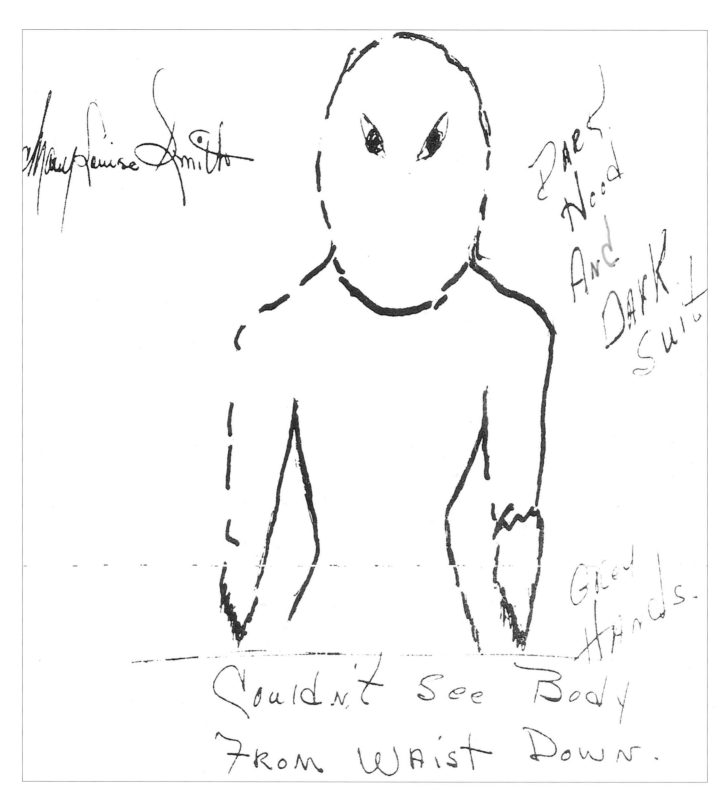

Drawing by Louise Smith, UFO abductee, of one of the entities which abducted her and two female friends in 1976

OUT-OF-THIS-WORLD SEX

The story of Antonio Villas Boas is one of many in which aliens are said to have had sex with human beings. There has been a spate of such encounters in recent years — particularly in Britain — and it is tempting to dismiss many of them as the work of fanciful imagination, wishful thinking, mental illness or simply a drunken episode.

As UFOlogist Philip Mantle puts it: 'Whether the cause or causes of their experiences come from Outer Space or "Inner Space" is a matter for research and further debate. The fact is that a growing number of people believe they have been taken away from their familiar surroundings and introduced to something so strange, so odd, that it often changes their outlook on life completely'.

Typical of these cases is that of mother-of-two Lynda Jones on 19 August 1979, on the banks of the River Mersey near Manchester. She was with her two children, aged 15 and 5, when the youngest shouted: 'Mum, the moon is coming towards us'.

Lynda looked up and saw an disc-shaped object spinning frisbee-like across the sky towards them. At first she thought it was an aircraft attempting to make a crash landing at nearby Manchester Airport. She told the children to lie flat and brace themselves for an explosion. Nothing happened.

She watched as the UFO dropped silently down behind an embankment. Grey and metallic, it seemed to be built of an intricate lattice-work of metal and measured about 18 metres/60 feet across. It hovered approximately 60 cm/2 feet off the ground.

'I took in everything around me', she said later, 'and thought: Oh my God, this is judgment day. I'm not ready for this'.

She turned and fled, grasping her children by the hand, but the UFO seemed to follow them. They ran all the way home, a journey which normally took ten minutes but on this occasion it took nearly an hour and a half – even running at full speed. The UFO appeared to be affecting the flow of time itself.

Subsequent regression analysis suggests that what actually happened was that she saw a figure emerge from the UFO. It seized her and laid her on a table in a room while six humanoids watched.

'I distinctly remember them putting something on my legs; it felt like pieces of ice. Bright lights were shone into my eyes'.

As with other female abductees, her menstrual cycle was affected for months afterwards. Strange marks began to appear on her body and, a few weeks later, she had a discharge. 'My GP said I'd had a miscarriage, but I had not been pregnant'.

Later examinations found scar tissue on her fallopian tubes.

An even more vivid tale comes from the town of Birstall, West Yorkshire. One night in 1981, tired mum Jane Murphy went to bed only to wake a few hours later in a strange room with a group of aliens who were approximately 2.5 metres/7 feet tall.

Completely naked, she was helped on to a table in the centre of the room and one of the figures approached her and either raped or seduced her — Murphy is unsure which word to use. She said later:

'I looked into his big, black eyes and knew that it was going to happen. Suddenly he was was lying on the table and I was lying on top of him. We were sort of embracing but lying very still. I noticed his smell. It wasn't very pleasant, not a human smell at all. Then we were having sex. It was the strangest sensation of all. We were lying together, not moving, but all the sensations of human sex were there.

'I couldn't even tell if he had any clothes on or not because I simply looked into his eyes. All I can remember is those gigantic black eyes. I didn't think about it as a physical act. I can't say that I was conscious of his penis because I wasn't. But inside, inside me it was all happening. At the time, I felt it was the best sex I had ever had. It seemed so strange lying on top of this stranger, not moving yet having sex and enjoying it'.

Close encounter with two UFO entities in Italy 1978 (top)   Interpretation of UFO event by Scottish artist Michael Buher, Scotland (bottom)

Afterwards, she was examined by other aliens who seemed to communicate by telepathy. Suddenly, in what appeared to be moments later, she was back in her own bed.

Jane Murphy wondered whether her experience had been a dream, but next morning when she rose to bathe, she found curious puncture marks where the aliens had injected her. She felt a strange sensation in the pit of her stomach, one she remembered from pregnancy, and was horrified when her menstrual cycle stopped. She required a course of powerful antibiotics to rid her of a curious infection which plagued her for months afterwards. She was not pregnant, but was subsequently tortured by dreams in which she gave birth to a blond, black-eyed alien.

Another sexual encounter is alleged to have taken place deep in the Essex countryside. Ted Johnson was driving down a deserted country road on 27 September 1985 when he saw a strange light gleaming at him in the distance.

'I saw the light and heard a low whistling sound,' he said later. 'The light became so bright it hurt my eyes. Then I was hit by a green light which knocked me to the ground, partially blinding me'.

As he scrambled to his feet, he saw a strangely dressed woman with large eyes, a small nose and a slit instead of a mouth. She seemed to be somehow glowing. Other humanoid shapes moved about in the darkness behind her.

Johnston was led into the craft where, he claims, they made love. 'She was naked and we had sex', he said. 'It was no different to human sex'.

Perhaps a clue to the mystery of these amazing tales can be gleaned from the words of UFO expert and author John Keel. He suspects certain individuals may be more susceptible to sightings or abductions than others. He says, 'Perhaps only certain types of people can see them at all. There are strange forces which are almost beyond our powers of comprehension'.

FIRE IN THE SKY

Two terrifying cases of alien abductions have tantalised scientists, psychologists and UFOlogists more than any others. One case — that of Barney and Betty Hill — is famous because it was the first UFO abduction to gain global attention. The second — the case of Travis Walton — is the most renowned of all, because it was the subject of a movie.

Both of these incidents occurred in the United States, where more research has been conducted into alien encounters than anywhere else. Both of these dramatic stories baffled students of the scientific and the psychic worlds. The experiences are many and varied. The explanations: nil.

Travis Walton's saga begins on the evening of 5 November 1975 as he and six other forestry workers were returning home to the town of Snowflake, Arizona, after a day's work in the great Sitgreave-Apache national park. He was in a pick-up truck with six of his colleagues, being driven by his best friend, forestry foreman Mike Rogers.

Suddenly, rounding a corner, Rogers slammed on the brakes. Ahead of them, just off the track, was a glowing, yellowish object hovering less than 5 metres/15 feet above a clearing. For a moment there was a stunned silence. Then Walton leaped from the truck and ran towards the clearing. His only aim was to get a better look at the UFO. But he was destined for an Encounter of the Third Kind — and beyond.

Walton recalled: 'The guys were calling out to me, "Get away from there, get back in the truck". But I guess that just egged me on. I was scared but I was showing off a bit, too'.

As the foolhardy forestry worker approached the ominously hovering UFO, a beam of blue light lifted him into the air and hurled him back onto the ground. His friends were to testify that 'a flash of blue and white light like a bolt of lightning' had emanated from the craft. Travis having ignored their shouted entreaties, the men in the truck raced off leaving their friend lying on the ground 'like a limp rag doll', according to Walton. Later, ashamed of themselves for having abandoned their friend, the six returned to the clearing. But the spacecraft had vanished as quickly as it had appeared. And so had Travis Walton.

The forestry crew reported the strange appearance and disappearance to police in Snowflake. Lawmen began to wonder whether or not the six had done away with Travis and covered up their crime with a hogwash story about aliens. A massive hunt was launched for him, with police combing every part of the national park and neighbouring areas. But they could find no trace of Walton, who had little money, no change of clothes and no transport.

Then, five days after Walton's vanishing act, his sister received a telephone call from him, from a call box in a nearby town. He was badly shaken but was unable to say what had occurred in the missing days. Police quizzed him to no avail. Only later, under hypnosis, was he able to reveal his astonishing story.
'We all saw the saucer that night. I was excited as the truck halted and I just jumped out and ran towards the glow. I felt no fear. Then something hit me. It was like the blow of an electric prod to my jaw and then everything went black. When I woke up I thought I was in hospital. I was on a table on my back and as I focused I saw three figures.

'It was weird. They weren't humans. They looked like foetuses to me, about 150 cm (five feet) tall, and they wore tight-fitting tan brown robes. Their skin was white like a mushroom but they had no clear features. I guess I panicked. I picked up a transparent tube and tried to smash it to use as a weapon, but it wouldn't break. I was petrified. I wanted to attack them, but they just scampered away. I was alone.

'Then another man suddenly appeared a few feet from me. He seemed human, but he just smiled at me through a kind of helmet, like a fish bowl. He led me through a corridor into another big bright room, where there was a high-backed chair in the centre of the room. There was a lever on one arm and buttons on the other. The man left as suddenly as he had arrived and I began to play with the buttons. I pushed the lever.

Betty and Barney Hill, abducted in 1961

'The scene outside suddenly changed. I felt we were moving. I knew we were in a spaceship. Then things went black again. When I woke I was shaky. I was on the highway. It was black but all the streets were lit up because just a few feet away was the flying saucer. I saw no one, and was still wearing my working clothes. I just ran. I recognised I was in a place a few miles from my home in Hever and called my sister.

'I know people won't believe me, that they'll call me a freak or a crackpot, but I was in their spaceship and I met those creatures'. That was Travis Walton's explanation for a five-day disappearance. He has never wavered from his story from that day.

In 1993 Walton's dramatic encounter with aliens was made into a major movie titled Fire In The Sky, starring James Garner. The actor said: 'If I hadn't believed Travis Walton's story implicitly after talking to him for many hours, I wouldn't have touched the project with a bargepole'.

Finally, consider the case of Betty and Barney Hill, regular 'Mr and Mrs USA', who were driving home from a Canadian holiday to their home in New Hampshire when their close encounter became one of the most sinister on record. It was certainly the first space-napping to receive world-wide publicity.

On the night of 19 September 1961 they stopped their car near Connecticut River Valley in the White Mountains of New Hampshire because a strange object — a ball as bright as a star — had apparently been following them for over an hour. They stopped the car to stare at the craft, Barney examining it through a pair of binoculars.

It was a sight that sent shivers of horror through him. He witnessed malevolent, man-shaped creatures with ice-blue, evil eyes, dressed in black jackets.

With Betty imploring him to get back into the car, he finally dragged himselfaway from the spell-binding scene. But then the mystery deepened. As they drove away, they noticed that they were about 55 km/35 miles further south than they had been when they stopped the car to look at the spacecraft. Both felt numb and confused, aware that in approximately an hour that had elapsed, something sinister had happened but not quite sure what. Neither could account for the missing time or distance.

Ten days later, the couple began to suffer severe physical pains and Betty began to have excruciating nightmares, dreaming of strange beings attacking her. Neither Barney nor Betty sought any publicity over their experience but, as their ailments persisted, they eventually sought the help of a psychiatrist, Dr Benjamin Simon. He conducted a series of regressions on the couple and, after six months of hypnotic sessions, unlocked their terrible secret.

Barney had not, after all, run back to the car. Under hypnosis, both of them admitted that they had entered the spaceship. There, they were both subjected to medical examination. They became human guinea pigs, as samples of teeth, flesh, hair, skin and nails were taken.

Betty, a social worker, was given what she realised had been a pregnancy test, with ova samples being drawn through a tube. Barney had samples of sperm extracted from his groin by means of a suction device.

Betty said the pain was terrible but that it went after another of the aliens rubbed his hands in front of her eyes, and told her that the hurt would go. Barney recalled much less except that he felt pain when his groin was examined, a pain that recurred when he got back home.

The couple were then shown a map of the heavens. Transcripts of their evidence under hypnosis was given to astronomer Marjorie Fish who located the aliens' supposed 'home planet' as being near the star Zeta Reticulii. The Hills picked up a book or chart aboard the spacecraft to take away as proof of their experience but the space visitors later took it back.

Dr Simon concluded that Barney and Betty Hill — neither of whom ever wavered in their accounts — had both been transported for medical examination, and that the UFO occupants had tried to wipe their memories clean of the two hours or so that they spent in their custody. They had not, however, been able to obliterate the eerie recollections from the deep recesses of the human mind.

CONCLUSION

THE 64-MILLION DOLLAR QUESTION

There have been thousands of sightings since Kenneth Arnold's 'flying saucers' first made headlines almost fifty years ago. It would be sceptical in the extreme to suggest every single account is a hoax, given the substantial evidence – in the form of radar contact and independent sightings in the air and on the ground – which supports them.

The central question for UFOlogists lies in identifying what exactly UFOs are. This task has generated more sci-fi books, films, television series, idle speculation and hot air than almost anything else in the 20th century.

There can be no doubt that the vast majority of supposed UFOs are naturally explainable phenomena. The planet Venus, whose movement across the sky is often visible to the naked eye, has proved to be behind many sightings.

Noctilucence, where clouds reflect sunlight from beyond the horizon, can create dazzling effects. Lenticular clouds – strange disc-shaped gatherings of water vapour in the upper atmosphere – have also been offered as explanations. Even the landing lights of a passenger jet can appear other-worldly to the naked eye given the right circumstances.

But these cannot serve for all UFOs. Some incidents cannot easily be explained. Indeed, this book has given numerous examples of sightings which seem to defy the most fundamental laws of physics. Lenticular clouds, for instance, do not appear as solid metallic blips on radar screens. Noctilucence cannot zap a fighter pilot's weapons system. The planet Venus does not travel across the sky at speeds of more than 1000 km/600 miles per hour.

Sightings by professional pilots are particularly convincing, especially since their visual reports can be attested to by radar and by observers on the ground. The Washington Flap is a prime example. Hundreds of people saw lights in the sky during that summer of 1952. The sightings were backed up by as many as three separate radar installations. And what explanation can there be for the photographs taken from the Almirante Saldanha research vessel in 1958? The object in the pictures was seen by 48 people and the developing and processing of the film was completed under the strictest possible supervision.

These sightings cannot be dismissed, unlike the many abduction stories which have surfaced since the late 1950s. There is still not a single abduction which has been verified by a credible witness who saw the alleged victim or victims enter the spacecraft. Nor has a single artifact from within the spacecraft been produced. Even Antonio Villas Boas, one of the most convincing abductees, says rather curiously that he was caught attempting to steal a small box from his alien hosts.

So who or what is responsible for UFOs? Assuming for the moment that they are not spontaneous hallucinations or the result of some natural phenomenon, the origins of which we are unaware — such as the Earth lights theory – then there are two possibilities. Either they originate on our planet or they are from somewhere else.

Some UFOs could indeed be experimental aircraft — the Betty Cash encounter springs immediately to mind. More likely perhaps is the suggestion that UFO stories may be deliberately circulated in order to cover up more sinister activities by governments and armed forces. The Rendlesham Forest incident could be a case in point. Was there a leak of radioactive material? Did a secret weapon turn maverick? Why were servicemen allowed to leak detailed information about events that night? Why did Whitehall say there were 'no defence implications'?

There could be no better way to muddy the waters of a potentially embarrassing incident than to blame the little green — or grey — men. This so-called Federal Hypothesis, which suggests governments are being behind the majority of UFOs, ties in with repeated sightings over secret military and nuclear sites.

FACT OR FICTION?: UFOs

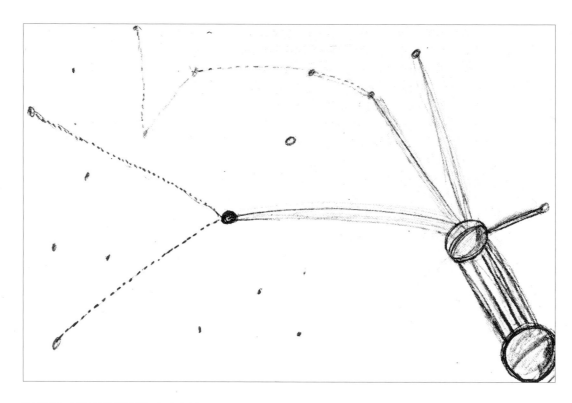

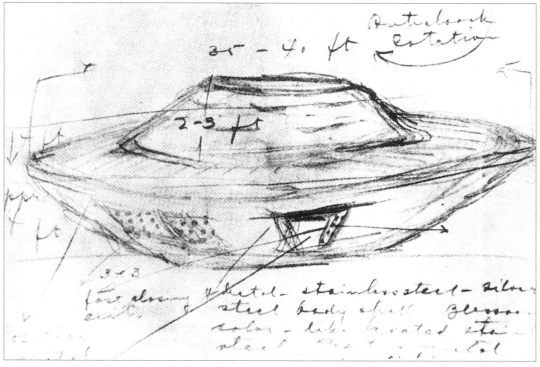

Star map drawn by Betty Hill during her abduction, in 1961 (top)   Steve Michalak's sketch of the UFO he encountered near Manitoba, Canada in 1967 (bottom)

<u>CONCLUSION</u>

A message sent into space

When these factors are taken on board, the dangers of accepting any UFO account at face value are immediately apparent. This central tenet of responsible UFOlogy is essential when we consider the possibility that unidentified flying saucers might originate from somewhere other than our own planet.

The evidence to support this extra-terrestrial hypothesis rests — assuming we discount abduction evidence on the grounds that most of it is unverifiable — on the technology apparently used by UFOs. Human pilots speak of them performing high-gee turns of up to 80 degrees which would kill any passenger, of 90 degree climbs and manoeuvres which can only be described as controlled, evasive action.

Speeds measured on radar can be anything up to escape velocity (around 40,200 km/25,000 miles per hour). There are also several reports of what appear to be mother ships docking with smaller craft high in the atmosphere. The suggestion from those who support the extra-terrestrial hypothesis is that UFOs are sophisticated space vehicles and if we cannot build machines like them, they must come from another planet, another time or perhaps even another dimension.

At this point, many writers on the subject allow their imagination to run away with them. The so-called ratchet effect comes into play, where each piece of 'evidence' thought to be positive is added to the case for extra-terrestrial involvement and everything that knocks the case down is quietly forgotten. There have been all sorts of conspiracy theories involving aliens: that the US government has access to alien technologies (hence the Stealth programme); that world leaders know the truth about UFOs and are hiding it from the public for fear of their reaction; that aliens are somehow protecting our planet from nuclear annihilation; that aliens are using human beings for genetic experiments.

Indeed, it is tempting to speculate that the post-war wave of UFO sightings is somehow linked to the detonation of the first atom bombs and the start of the space race. Perhaps, goes the theory, our intergalactic neighbours were concerned that we might become a threat to them. This was the central plot of the classic 1950s sci-fi movieThe Day The Earth Stood Still, when a flying saucer from another star system lands in Washington to persuade world leaders of their folly in pursuing the arms race.

Today, from what we suspect to be the true nature of space and time, we know were such craft to exist, they might just as easily come from our own future as from another galaxy.

Most researchers on the NASA-funded Search For Extraterrestrial Intelligence (SETI), which combs the sky for transmissions from other worlds, believe initial contacts, when they come, will be in the form of data exchanges.

For example, there may be vast bodies of digital knowledge flashed across space to prepare both sides for an eventual meeting. It should also be noted that despite thousands of UFO sightings in recent years, SETI and other similar projects have yet to find any intelligent radio sources anywhere in our galaxy.

This does not alter the fact that UFOs most definitely do exist. Some may be experimental craft, wayward missiles or freaks of nature; the true stories emerge about these events years later. Other sightings remain inexplicable.

Most rational human beings keep an open mind on the possibility that beings from other worlds or times have visited this tiny, water-covered globe 150 million km/93 million miles from a very ordinary star on the very edge of a very ordinary galaxy.